MISPLACED BLAME

The Real Roots of Population Growth

Alan Thein Durning
Christopher D. Crowther

With research assistance by
Yoram Bauman

NEW Report No. 5
July 1997

Northwest Environment Watch
Seattle, Washington

NEW thanks editor and typesetter Ellen W. Chu and reviewers Judith Jacobsen, Charles Langdon, Jacqueline Hamilton, Mike A. Males, Thomas M. Power, Howard Wineberg, and William Frey for their skilled contributions. We thank Mike A. Males in particular for many hours of data analysis, without which the book would not be the same. We also thank for their dedicated assistance interns Nicholas Dankers, Paige Pluymers, and especially Steve Sullivan and volunteers Peter Carlin, Norman Kunkel, Lyn McCollum, Ellen Pyle, Marilyn Roy, Sandra Singler, David Skavdahl, Scott Stevens, and Darrel Weiss. We thank cover photographer Marita Holdaway of Benham Studio and Gallery, models Toni Lucas and Leah, and back cover photographer Michael Wewer. NEW is grateful to its board of directors: Lester R. Brown of Washington, D.C.; Sandi Chamberlain of Victoria, B.C.; Aaron Contorer of Kirkland, Wash.; Alan Thein Durning, Sandra Blair Hernshaw, and Tyree Scott of Seattle; and Rosita Worl of Juneau. NEW expresses its profound appreciation to Donna Morton, outgoing communications director, for three years of excellent service.

Financial support for this book was provided by the Lazar Foundation, Weeden Foundation, Wilburforce Foundation, and contributors to Northwest Environment Watch. These include more than 1,400 individuals and the Bullitt Foundation, C. S. Fund, Nathan Cummings Foundation, Ford Foundation, William and Flora Hewlett Foundation, Henry P. Kendall Foundation, John D. and Catherine T. MacArthur Foundation, Merck Family Fund, Surdna Foundation, True North Foundation, Turner Foundation, and an anonymous Canadian foundation. Views expressed are the authors' and do not necessarily represent those of Northwest Environment Watch or its directors, officers, staff, or funders. Northwest Environment Watch is a 501(c)(3) tax-exempt organization.

NEW staff: Peg Cheng, communications director; Rhea Connors, office manager and volunteer coordinator; Alan Thein Durning, executive director; Kyle Halmrast, development and outreach director; John Ryan, research director; and Steve Sullivan, development and outreach assistant.

This book was printed in Vancouver, B.C., using vegetable-based ink and recycled paper. Text: 100 percent postconsumer waste, bleached with hydrogen peroxide. Cover: 50 percent preconsumer waste, bleached with hydrogen peroxide. Design by Visible Images, Seattle.

Excerpts from this book may be printed in periodicals with written permission from Northwest Environment Watch, 1402 Third Avenue, Suite 1127, Seattle, WA 98101-2118; tel.: (206) 447-1880; fax: (206) 447-2270; e-mail: nwwatch@igc.apc.org; Web: http://www.speakeasy.org/new

TABLE OF CONTENTS

MISCONCEPTIONS

T HINK OF YOUR EARLIEST childhood memory.

Now hear Paige Latin's. "I was about two. It was in the washroom of my home, where I lived with my mum and dad. I remember the washroom. It was yellow. I don't have a face for the man's body, but I have the body and ..." Her voice drops off. "He sexually abused me. He was the first of many." Paige is talking to a score of fifteen- and sixteen-year-olds at a secondary school in Vancouver, B.C. Her talk is part of a personal campaign to raise awareness about sexual abuse in order to prevent one of its worst consequences: prostitution. She doesn't intend to, but she is also slowing population growth. A second major consequence of child sexual abuse is a high birthrate.

Think of your father.

Now listen to social worker Charlie Langdon testifying before the legislature in Olympia, Washington. "What's really sad, Representative Boldt, is that in this state, the last figures show that only 54 percent of fathers are documented. The paternity was only established in 54 percent of births to school-age mothers. So there's no way to get child support, and that's one reason so many kids live in poverty."

He doesn't intend to, but, like Paige Latin, he is slowing
population growth. Youth poverty is the single largest cause
of high birthrates and early childbearing in North America.

Think of a housing development going in near your
hometown.

Now listen to Republican representative Chuck Carpenter in Salem, Oregon. "My constituents have expressed
a lot of concerns about growth. Increasingly, they are paying for the additional schools and the infrastructure. Taxpayers should know the true costs" of urban expansion.
Carpenter has introduced a bill into Oregon's legislature
requiring a "taxpayer impact statement" for development
of rural land. He doesn't intend to, but he too is slowing
population growth. Subsidies to new suburban development artificially lower the price of housing for middle-
and upper-class migrants, inducing additional migration.

Paige Latin, Charlie Langdon, and Chuck Carpenter—
disparate in most of their life experiences and outlooks—
are on the front lines of efforts to slow population growth
in the Pacific Northwest and, by extension, North America.
And they do not even know it. For reasons entirely their
own, they have homed in on three of the seldom-noted
roots of population growth: child abuse, child poverty, and
subsidies to suburban development. Some people are dig-
ging up other roots, too, including the starving of family-
planning and abortion services and ill-conceived immigration laws.

Unfortunately, other people are unwittingly speeding
population growth, by acting (again, for their own reasons)
in ways that reinforce the causes. And many people—most
of us, perhaps—hold misconceptions about population and

the driving forces behind it. The misconceptions themselves may well be the largest barriers to slowing growth.

These misconceptions include the belief that population growth in developing countries causes most of the world's environmental problems but that population growth is not an issue in North America. They include the belief that newcomers moving into an area boost the local tax base. They include the belief that most immigrants arrive illegally. They include the belief that family planning is the cure for population growth, wherever it occurs. The misconceptions include the belief that teen parenting is the cause of much poverty in America—that if only teenagers would practice personal responsibility, they would escape poverty for themselves and their children. They include the belief that generous immigration quotas in North America benefit developing nations. And they include the belief that lots of public money goes to the poor through welfare programs while North Americans who are not poor pay their own way.

These misconceptions leave us all misplacing blame. We blame the poor, the young, women, and immigrants for our social ills; we blame poor nations for our planetary woes. We blame too much of population growth on the Third World and blame population growth for too large a share of nature's and society's ailments.

Make no mistake: population growth is among the defining challenges of our era. Worldwide, it exacerbates problems ranging from dwindling topsoil to overcrowded classrooms. And widespread public concern about our growing numbers led to the landmark United Nations Conference on Population and Development in Cairo in

1994, where the international community made a commitment. It resolved to provide all the world's women with the means to choose their own reproductive future, thereby establishing the conditions for stabilizing human numbers.

Unfortunately, public concern about population, though wide, is not terribly deep, so this commitment remains largely rhetorical. The heart of the matter is that population growth, like most global problems, is best addressed locally. And local solutions require local knowledge, local actors, and local motives—motives grounded in local values.

So this book, which aims to help slow population growth, examines that growth in one discrete place: the Pacific Northwest bioregion, which stretches from Prince William Sound, Alaska, to the redwood coast of California—along a shoreline once cloaked in nearly continuous rain forests—and spreads inland to headwaters as far east as the continental divide (see map inside front cover). Defined as the watersheds of rivers flowing into the Pacific through North America's temperate rain forest zone, this bioregion encompasses the Canadian province of British Columbia and the American states of Idaho, Oregon, and Washington plus southeastern Alaska, northwestern California, and western Montana.

With a population of 15 million and a gross regional product exceeding $300 billion, the Pacific Northwest is a natural proving ground for a new, Cairo-inspired approach to population. The Northwest is the most ecologically intact part of the industrial world, and it is home to people who are among the best educated and the most environmentally informed.

This place has the opportunity to demonstrate a population approach that averts growth by activating bedrock North American values: protecting vulnerable individuals while nurturing the health of communities. After all, *population* is nothing but a four-syllable word for "us." So policy that addresses population must be built on the foundation of each person's inherent dignity, worth, and potential. Affirming this principle, *Misplaced Blame* is about slowing the growth of human numbers by better caring for people, both because that's the only ethical option and because it's the only option that can work.

The Pacific Northwest is also a test case of international significance because it has far more than its share of population growth. Regional growth outstrips national and global growth rates. Many longtime northwesterners are disturbed by this silent surge, pained by the incremental losses they have watched come with it: deteriorating air and water quality; crowded streets, parks, and wildlands; and rising housing costs. Yet most northwesterners assume that nothing can be done.

They are mistaken.

Growth would be inevitable were its causes simply the exercise of basic human rights such as reproductive freedom or freedom of movement. But recent growth has not come purely from free choices, consciously made. It has also come from chance, ignorance, and failures in government leadership. Specifically, population growth in the Northwest has five roots: child poverty, child sexual abuse, inadequate family-planning services, subsidies to domestic migration, and ill-guided immigration policy. Attack these roots, weed them out, and growth will slow dramatically.

Already, some signs are heartening. Birthrates have declined during the 1990s across North America. The churning displacement of people and communities that has dominated this century in North America is abating slightly. Mobility is slowing, and more people are putting down roots. International migration into North America has probably peaked and begun to diminish. And these hopeful signs have emerged despite the lack of concerted public attention to population growth. What might be possible if we tried?

ROOT 1

CHILD POVERTY

OLYMPIA, WASHINGTON, January 23, 1997. Carrie Coppinger Carter, a law student and mother of one from rural Whatcom County, Washington, is testifying on a welfare reform bill before the legislature. "I am a former teenage parent," she says, addressing chairwoman Suzette Cook and her colleagues on the House Committee on Children and Family Services. She reads the bill's second paragraph aloud: "It is the public policy of the state . . . to discourage teen pregnancy by unwed parents as an action that is destructive to society." She raises her eyes to Representative Cook and says, "My daughter is not destructive to society."

In the back of the hearing room, Charlie Langdon, a stocky transplanted easterner with a ruddy complexion and a shock of white hair, is suppressing a cheer. Awaiting his turn to testify, he can't keep himself from whispering running commentary on the day's proceedings. "Carrie's great. She's one of our best speakers. She milked cows all the way through high school to help support herself." Charlie is on a first-name basis with many of the former and present teenage mothers in Washington State. He came out of retirement to direct a struggling nonprofit outfit that helps them. Called Advancing Solutions to Adolescent Pregnancy (ASAP), it organizes programs for pregnant and parenting teenagers.

Unfortunately, Charlie's on an uphill climb—more like a winter ascent of nearby Mount Rainier. The United States is in the midst of a national witch hunt aimed at teenage mothers, blaming them for corrupting the moral fiber of the nation, bearing most of the country's criminals and juvenile delinquents, causing poverty, and soaking up public dollars to support idle lives.[1]

Decades of research in the social sciences debunk these claims, but no matter. Much of the public believes them, and in politics, perceptions are reality. So the federal government has rewritten the rules on public assistance, rescinding the principle that everyone who resides legally in this country is entitled to assistance when she or he falls on hard times. The federal government has slashed budgets for helping people who become poor and delegated most authority to the states, giving them about a year to rewrite their own welfare laws. The welfare overhaul drafted by Representative Cook singles out young mothers for special censure, promising to cut them off the rolls. The bill also requires almost all adult welfare recipients to work or do community service. It tells young mothers to go back to their parents' homes. And it limits aid to a cumulative total of five years per person.[2]

Teenage parenting is a product of social policies in North America that abandon young families to poverty. Blaming teen mothers for their poverty is especially convoluted because, although many teen moms do live in poverty, they're not poor because they're moms. They live in poverty because they are poor—and have been long before they became mothers. Eighty-three percent of American teenage mothers were poor before they became mothers.[3]

And poor women who become mothers as teens do no worse for themselves than poor women who become mothers in their twenties. Except among mothers younger than fifteen, teen parenting is not the core problem. Indeed, for most of history, many women have started their families in their teenage years. Poverty is the real problem, showing up in all the sad statistics about teen parenting: high poverty rates, high dropout rates, high substance abuse rates, high child abuse rates, high rates of crime and delinquency. If you're poor, there is no good time to have a family.[4]

If population growth were a major public issue, it might well be blamed on teen mothers too. After all, in the Northwest between 1980 and 1995, 20 percent of natural increase in population (births minus deaths) consisted of births to mothers younger than twenty. But this observation misses the point. The truth is that the poverty responsible for teen births also deserves blame for much population growth—growth due to earlier childbearing and to increased childbearing overall.[5]

Outside its poorest groups, the Northwest does not have a high birthrate. The 2-child family has been the regional norm for a quarter century. After the baby boom years of the 1950s and early 1960s, when typical northwestern women were having between 3 and 4 children each, family size decreased swiftly. In 1972, the total fertility rate per woman came to relative stability and has remained there, hovering around 2 children per woman in the Northwest states and 1.6 children per woman in British Columbia.[6]

The reason the Northwest states have higher fertility rates than B.C. is not that middle-class Americans want larger families than middle-class Canadians. It is that more Canadians are middle class—or, more precisely, that British Columbians do not tolerate child poverty on the scale that exists in American parts of the bioregion. (Of course, British Columbians do live with child poverty on a scale that is intolerable to most other affluent societies.) The norm among northwesterners who are not poor is families with fewer than two children—a fertility rate that would eventually lead to a modest and beneficial reduction in population, were it not for people moving in from elsewhere.[7]

As economic inequalities have expanded in the United States since 1979, the timing of childbearing has become a class issue. Just as income prospects have diverged, so have childbearing patterns. The haves in the new economy wait until after graduate school to have children; the have-nots begin during high school. This divergence is something new. For generations, American fertility was dominated by early marriage and childbearing, often beginning in the teenage years. Since 1970, the middle and upper classes have begun to delay starting their families. The poor, meanwhile, have continued on the traditional schedule.[8]

Here's the bottom line for the Northwest's population: roughly one-third of births in the Pacific Northwest simply would not occur if the bioregion eliminated poverty; that's how much poverty boosts the birthrate. Poverty generates most births to teens and also increases fertility among nonteens. Women who live in poverty have about twice as many children, on average, as more affluent women. They do so not because they are foolish or ignorant, as common misconceptions hold, but because they are playing the hand they were dealt as best they can. Their entire life experience confirms they will not go far in the new, fiercely competitive global economy. They do not actively seek pregnancy, but they are less aggressive than women who are not poor in attempting to prevent it. They are less careful with contraception, and they accept pregnancy when it happens. At least, they reason, they can be good mothers, raise good children, and fill their lives with the challenges and rewards of having a family. In a money-mad world, motherhood is one role they cannot be denied.[9]

THE HEARING ROOM is getting more crowded as the morning progresses. Representative Cook is cutting speakers off at precisely three minutes, so there's little time to comment on the 161-page bill. Three former welfare mothers testify against different aspects of the legislation. Linda Stone from Spokane, chair of a statewide hunger coalition, notes that federal reform has already cut food stamps—the safety net beneath the safety net—by almost $100 million a year in Washington alone. She calls on the committee to follow Oregon's lead and increase welfare grants to mitigate cuts in food stamps.

Charlie is nodding his agreement. "This is legislation that attempts to address the problem of poverty by reducing payments to poor people." Changes in federal law have slashed $300 million from Washington's annual funding for social programs—part of a national cutback that is reducing income to 10 percent of American families, most of them desperately poor—and these changes come after a

long history of welfare cuts. Since 1969, the average welfare grant in Washington State has fallen from 100 percent
to 44 percent of the state's official "standard of need," cur-
rently $1,252 a month for a family of three.[10]

With the typical $546-per-month grant, the single
mother of two is supposed to cover everything from rent
to birthday presents. And Washington, like California and
Alaska, is a relatively generous state; Oregon, Montana, and
especially Idaho write smaller checks. Yet in none of these
states does the combination of food stamps and cash lift a
family even to the U.S. federal poverty line—the lowest
poverty standard of any industrial democracy. British Columbia makes larger grants: the same single mother of two
in Vancouver, B.C., would receive a monthly check for
Can$969 (about U.S.$727), along with refunds of the federal sales tax, much more assistance for child care, and full
coverage for dental and eye care. And B.C. provides full
medical coverage to all residents. Still, B.C.'s family security programs for children are minimal compared with those
of European nations.[11]

The welfare system, Charlie says, does need reform.
But the legislation before the committee is largely welfare
repeal. Residents of the state will no longer be entitled to
financial support when they are poor. "If you need $10 to
survive," he says, "you were guaranteed $4 on welfare. Under
the new system, you're not guaranteed two cents."

TEEN BIRTHS ARE A SMALL PART of the Pacific
Northwest's population growth. The growth overall is
massive: during the 1990s, the Northwest's population has

increased by 2.16 percent per year, nearly twice the North American rate and almost 50 percent faster than global population. British Columbia, Idaho, Oregon, and Washington—the four jurisdictions that account for 93 percent of the region's populace—consistently rank in the top ten for annual population growth among North American states and provinces.[12]

This growth is historically sudden: population in the Pacific Northwest first topped 1 million in 1880, and it took 25 years to add the second million, but as the twentieth century progressed, the million marks flew by ever more swiftly (see Figure 1). By mid-1997, the regional head count had reached 15 million, and it was swelling by another million every 40 months.[13]

Population is not evenly distributed across the region. More than 60 percent of northwesterners live within 60 miles of Interstate 5 (and its Canadian equivalent, Route 99), the highway that runs from Portland, Oregon, through Seattle, Washington, to Vancouver, B.C. In sheer numbers, most growth is accreting along this strip of pavement, although sunnier inland places, especially around Boise, Idaho, Kelowna, B.C., and Missoula, Montana, have shown some of the highest growth rates in recent years.[14]

In the period between 1985 and 1995 alone, northwesterners added 2.6 million to their ranks, roughly as many people as live in greater Seattle. This increase was larger than in any prior ten-year period, and growth is not slowing. Official projections forecast a year-2000 regional population almost 3 million higher than the 1990 count (see Figure 2).[15]

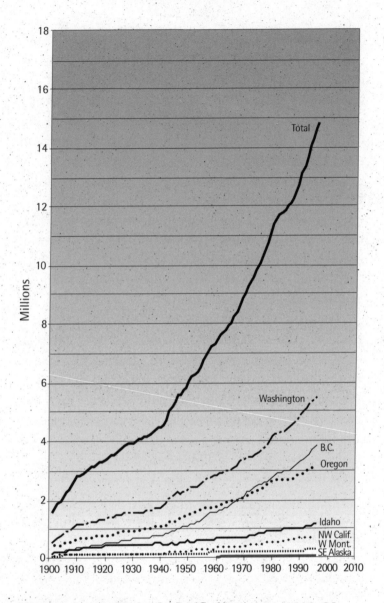

Figure 1. Population in the Pacific Northwest, 1900–96
Northwest population has doubled since 1960.
Sources: see endnote 13.

The Northwest's growth is part of a global population explosion that, for all its international significance, remains almost invisible in North American politics. Those born since 1950 make up the 2,000th generation of anatomically modern human beings, but no generation has been so large. For the first 1,350 generations, the number of people worldwide did not rise above 5 million, roughly the population of Washington State. It took until the 1,875th generation for population to top 100 million and until the 1,990th generation to reach 1 billion. Now there are almost 6 billion people, and the number is growing by another billion every dozen years.[16]

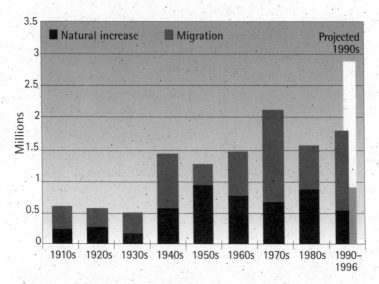

Figure 2. Migration and Natural Increase by Decade, Pacific Northwest, 1900–2000

Northwest population is surging in the 1990s.

Note: *includes B.C., Idaho, Oregon, and Washington.*

Sources: *see endnote 15.*

By ecological measures, the dominance of our species is dumbfounding. We have produced far more protoplasm—living tissue—than any other species ever. We make use of or degrade one-fourth of the plant matter that grows each year, along with one-third of the water that falls as rain on inhabited regions. These facts testify to our formidable problem-solving powers. Members of our species are now in the process of ascertaining the precise age of the universe, of deciphering the human genetic code, and of digitizing the world's libraries and moving them through telephone cables.[17]

Yet progress is proving difficult to sustain because success on the current model has worrisome consequences. The damage we cause the nonhuman realm—and ultimately ourselves—is as dumbfounding as our planetary dominance. Human enterprise has thinned the protective ozone layer and altered global climate. We have degraded or destroyed two-thirds of the world's forests and three-fourths of its grasslands; rewritten the chemistry of air, water, and even living things; and are now sentencing species to extinction at a rate exceeding one per hour. Our own bodies are not sacrosanct: they each contain some 500 chemicals that did not exist in 1900.[18]

Population growth is a major contributor to these problems, but it is not the root cause, as some of its most zealous critics imply. There is no one root cause. Rather, the pressures of population growth are unfolding along with other pressures, such as polluting technologies and inefficient infrastructure, heavy resource consumption among the fortunate, market economies blind to ecological value, and lack of public awareness.

Responsibility for the lion's share of damage to the life-giving systems of the Earth must be laid at the feet of North Americans and others in industrial societies. The United States, with one-twentieth of world population, consumes one-third or more of the world's paper, plastic, computers, and cars; one-fourth of the world's energy, copper, and aluminum; one-fifth of the world's beef; and one-sixth of the world's grain and steel.[19]

Certainly, population growth is a problem of the first order, especially where that growth is made up of people who use lots of resources, as in the Pacific Northwest. In the Northwest, burgeoning numbers of people are putting pressures on both human and natural environments. As population grows, so does the demand for high-environmental-impact commodities such as cars, energy, and buildings. As population grows, so does ecological damage. Growth worsens the contamination of drinking water supplies, augments air pollution, speeds urban sprawl, overfills roads and sewers, crowds beaches and parks, and imposes ever more stress on already embattled forests and rivers.

Comparing rates of change in population and in closely related environmental indicators provides a rough gauge of population growth's role in the Northwest. Take urban sprawl. Population grew half as quickly as developed land area in greater Seattle during the 1970s and 1980s, so population growth could be blamed for about half the sprawl. On these grounds, from 1982 to 1992, population growth caused 41 percent of land development in western Montana, 47 percent in Idaho, and 71 percent in Oregon. Or take car traffic. Population growth accounted for 45 percent of the increase in total miles driven in Idaho, Oregon, and Washington between 1957 and 1993. The remainder came because driving more than doubled per person.[20]

By similar reasoning, population growth is responsible for most of the growth in four other important, quantifiable areas: consumption of energy, use of residential water, generation of solid waste, and emissions of heat-trapping carbon dioxide. On these measures, per capita environmental impacts in the region have stabilized. Yet all four measures are climbing with population.[21]

Other factors are at work as well. The number of households is especially important because the household, rather than the individual, is often the basic unit of consumption. Houses, automobiles, and other ecologically significant commodities are usually shared within households. And large households usually have opportunities to use such commodities more efficiently than small households. So when households shrink, as in the Northwest, resource consumption increases, regardless of total population. Households have shrunk 16 percent since 1970, to 2.6 members in the United States, because adults are having fewer children and spending less of their lives married.[22]

Still, this book concerns itself primarily with numbers of people, not with numbers of suburban acres developed, per capita tons of natural resources consumed, jobs, cars, households, or dollars in the regional economy. An increase in any of these numbers is ecologically significant, but all move somewhat independently. Indeed, viewing population growth as a surrogate for all the other kinds of growth is another case of misplaced blame.

Over this century, natural increase has contributed slightly less to Northwest population than migration (persons moving to the Northwest minus persons leaving). Since 1980, for example, planned and unplanned births to adult and teenage women have accounted for 42 percent of new northwesterners, while domestic and international migration has accounted for 58 percent (see Figure 3). Policymakers can take actions that slow growth from each of these causes—causes that have added 3.3 million to regional population since 1980.[23]

Yet natural increase is the ultimate, global problem; migration simply shifts the population burden from one place to another. So a Northwest population strategy that aims for international leadership ought to put special emphasis

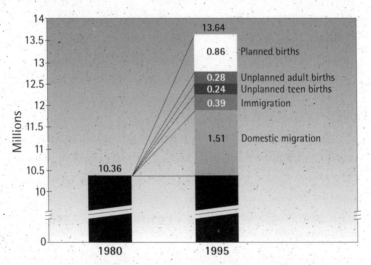

Figure 3. Population and Components of Growth, Pacific Northwest, 1980–95
Northwest population grew by more than 3 million in the last 15 years, roughly the population of Oregon.
Note: includes B.C., Idaho, Oregon, and Washington.
Sources and definitions: see endnote 23.

on slowing natural increase—a tall order but altogether possible. After all, some 36 percent of births in the Northwest result from accidental, unplanned pregnancies, and a vastly disproportionate share of these births are among poor women, especially poor young women. Better family-planning approaches can help (see "Root 3"), but alleviating poverty would help the most.[24]

CHARLIE LANGDON is at the microphone. He exchanges some banter with Representative Cook, then launches into his testimony. He speaks quickly, with a hint of Long Island in his voice: "Here's some background on teen pregnancy and parenting that calls into question the rhetoric that led to the federal reforms in welfare. There were two assumptions that were false," Charlie argues. "One was that we have an epidemic of teen births. The facts are that per capita teen births are lower now than they were in 1970, 1950, 1890, or 1850."

Teen birthrates in the Northwest are slightly lower than the continental average, thanks to lower-than-average poverty, and despite a late 1980s upturn, they are far below the rates of past decades. In 1994, 5 percent of female teenagers in the Northwest states gave birth, as did 2 percent of B.C. teens. Two-thirds of these women were eighteen or nineteen years old. The same year, every tenth baby born in the Northwest—some 18,900 infants—had a teenage mother; few of these babies were born in B.C.[25]

Several committee members are looking down or gazing around the room. Charlie charges ahead. Young families, whether with one parent or two, lack much-needed social supports. They are physically isolated because the Northwest's high residential mobility and dispersed, car-dependent communities leave them in neighborhoods full of people who do not know or trust one another. They have less extended family to call on for help because clans are strewn across the nation. Few families can afford to have one parent at home full time with the children, and few good part-time jobs are available. "More than half of twelve- to fifteen-year-olds in the United States," Charlie points out, "do not live with their biological father."

Charlie has almost run through his three minutes, and it's clear that beneath her gracious exterior, Representative Cook is eager to get him away from the microphone. He knows too much. "Charlie, would you provide your written testimony to staff?"

"I will."

"Thank you for coming today."

"May I conclude?" he presses his advantage.

"Very quickly. Your time is almost up."

The second misconception that has led welfare reform astray, Charlie says, talking even faster now, is about the fathers of children born to teen mothers. They aren't class-mates from homeroom. "If every high school male in America were entirely celibate, two-thirds of children born to mothers under eighteen would still be born. Most of the fathers are adults, but welfare reform is proceeding as if these children were conceived by immaculate conception."

Representative Cook is reaching for her microphone, preparing to cut Charlie off, so he concludes: "If we don't get some kind of support from these fathers, we're going to have another generation of teen parents coming up."

The chairwoman thanks him and begins calling on the next speaker, but a colleague taps her shoulder. "Oh," she says, a trace of frustration in her voice. "There are some questions." Charlie has won a few more minutes.

The first questioner asks how much is known about the identity of the men who father children with school-age mothers. It's exactly what Charlie wanted to talk about. Men in their twenties father two and a half times as many babies with high school–age girls as do high school–age boys. They father four times as many babies with junior high school–age girls as do junior high boys. Normal teen births, in other words, are actually adult-teen births and have been since record keeping began in the United States in 1921. Just 54 percent of these fathers' names are recorded on birth certificates in Washington.[26]

Representative Mary Lou Dickerson asks, "Charlie, it's often difficult to get the teenage mothers to identify who the fathers are. Why is that?"

Charlie says, "She's afraid she's going to lose the guy. The father of the child represents some kind of a future for a young girl who's got no future at all. She comes out of an abusive situation. She's moved a lot. She's lived in poverty. She's not successful in school. All of a sudden, an older guy comes along and he's her way out. And he says to her, 'If you identify me as the father, I'm gone.'" Nine times out of ten, she will lose him anyway, but not for a year or two.

BIRTHS TO TEENAGE GIRLS are strands in a larger web. They are manifestations of high rates of child poverty, which result from a polarizing private-sector economy and the public sector's failure to shelter young families from its impacts.

The globalization of commerce and the advance of technology are reordering workplaces, driving up incomes for the most skilled workers, driving down incomes for most others. This new economy amplifies the rewards for the winners and whittles away at the concession prizes for the losers. The median real earnings of high school graduates who attain no further education dropped 30 percent for men and 20 percent for women between 1972 and 1994; median real earnings for high school dropouts, meanwhile, plummeted. Black high school dropouts in 1994 earned half what black high school dropouts did in 1972. In the late 1960s, the American minimum wage was livable: a full-time worker could support a family of three above the poverty line. In the 1990s, even after the minimum wage increased in 1996, a similar worker could labor 40 hours a week, 52 weeks a year, and still fall 15 percent short of the poverty line.[27]

Disparities in income are widening: the United States is now the least equitable of industrial countries. More than half of American households had lower real incomes in 1990 than in 1973, yet the richest households reaped huge increases. Indeed, virtually all new wealth created in the United States between 1983 and 1989—the last period for which data are available—accrued to the top fifth of households. In 1989, 1 percent of U.S. households owned two-fifths of the country's wealth, a degree of concentration not seen since 1929.[28]

Canada has experienced the same polarizing forces in its economy but, impressively, has offset them through

progressive tax and spending policies, preventing the hol-
lowing out of the middle class that the United States has
experienced. After taxes and transfer payments, Canada's income distribution stayed essentially the same from 1967 to
1993. And throughout, the Canadian middle class has made
up the same share of the population, roughly 45 percent.[29]

This accomplishment explains how B.C. has largely
avoided the fraying of the social fabric evident in the Northwest states, where homicide, suicide, and other violent
crimes surged upward in the late 1980s and early 1990s,
especially among young people. Child abuse and child
sexual abuse increased, too, as did drug and alcohol use.
Economic and physical insecurity have fueled sales of millions of house alarms, car alarms, cellular phones, and fire-
arms. And insecurity has fueled explosive growth in two
specialty construction trades: building gated compounds
for the rich and prisons for the poor.[30]

Yet in both nations, children are particularly disadvan-
taged. In the Northwest states, 14.7 percent of children
live below the federal poverty line. Oregon falls exactly on
the average; the rates are higher than average in Washington (15.0 percent), northwestern California (16.0 percent),
and western Montana (18.5 percent) and lower than average in Idaho (12.3 percent) and southeast Alaska (9.1 percent). Then there's B.C.'s 21 percent child poverty rate by
the Canadian standard, which translates roughly to a 10
percent child poverty rate by the American standard. And
all these child poverty rates compare badly to Scandinavia's
3 percent and 7 percent in France and Germany.[31]

Children are the poorest age group in North America.
Overall, 40 percent of American poor are children;

children make up 48 percent of the chronically poor, people in poverty all year long. The United States has the highest child poverty by far, and the least effective safety net for children, of any industrial democracy. Far better, but still third worst among industrial democracies, is Canada. In Ireland, Israel, the United Kingdom, France, and seven smaller European nations, government assistance lifts more than half of poor children out of poverty. In the United States, government assistance lifts 17 percent of poor children out of poverty; in Canada, the figure is 40 percent. (In contrast, Social Security and other programs for American seniors move more than half of those over 65 out of poverty.)[32]

Sara Mosler, writing in the *New Yorker* in September 1995, surveyed the abandonment of children to these wretched circumstances and concluded, "Maybe America, for all its prating about family values, hates its children."[33]

The current round of welfare reforms has been the latest evidence of public indifference to children. These reforms have largely consisted of requiring increased work in exchange for public assistance. The intense popular appeal of this idea, evident in poll after poll, stems from the widely held misconceptions that poor people are poor because they won't work and that working people don't have to worry about becoming poor. The facts belie this notion: half of poor adults have paid jobs, and paid work provides half the income for poor families, twice what welfare checks do. But those paid jobs don't pay enough: in every Northwest state, more than one-third of poor children live in families where at least one parent works all year long. Four out of five adult welfare recipients who do not have paid jobs are caring for their young children.[34]

Meanwhile, almost one-third of adult welfare recipients nationwide are disabled parents or parents of disabled children; a study in Washington State found unremediated learning disabilities among more than one-third of adult welfare recipients. More than half of families that fall into poverty climb back out again in less than a year. The most common reasons for falling into poverty are divorce and unemployment.[35]

There are, no doubt, welfare recipients with every imaginable undesirable attribute, and a small segment of the poor stay poor and receive public assistance for many years. But there are also millionaires who cheat on their taxes and major corporations that poison public waterways for decades while receiving government subsidies. Mostly, welfare is a disability program combined with a program of minimal supplements to the incomes of poor working parents of young children. Now, thanks to welfare reform, these parents will have to work even harder, and outside the home. Many of them, no doubt, will go to work in the entry-level industry most open to poor women—child care—where they will help raise other mothers' children instead of their own.

Statistically, teen births are an open-and-shut case. They are a function of disadvantage—not godless immorality, not youthful irresponsibility, not sex-soaked television shows or rock lyrics, not sex education run amok, not corrupting peer pressure, not the loss of family values, not welfare's supposed incentives to breed—not any of the myths of the left-right war of words.[36]

Teen births are mistakenly blamed for poverty so often that it's worth laying this myth to rest. If teen births caused poverty (along with a long list of other social ills), as nearly everyone except the researchers who study the matter seems to believe, then the few teens who give birth and are not poor would be expected to fall into poverty. They do not. And poor teens who avoid parenting would be expected to escape poverty. They do not.[37]

If teen births caused poverty, then changes in the teen birthrate should predict changes in the poverty rate, but they do just the opposite. For 25 years, it's been possible to predict the teen birthrate in the United States with 90 percent accuracy simply from the previous decade's child poverty rate: poor nine-year-olds become pregnant eighteen-year-olds.[38]

Consider this study. Take dozens of pairs of sisters close in age and similar in every way except that one sister in each pair starts her family as a teenager, and the other starts hers in her twenties. Then monitor what happens to the sisters and their children. If early childbearing caused poverty, delinquency, welfare dependency, or any other undesirable attribute, there ought to be differences in these attributes between the children of the teen moms and those of the twenty-something moms. This study has been done; no differences were found. Poverty is the problem, and all the fuss about babies having babies is a distraction.[39]

The poverty-teen birth relationship is clear not only across time but across space. Adolescents from the poorest neighborhoods in King County, Washington, are nearly four times as likely to give birth as those from rich neighborhoods. Affluent white teens do get pregnant, although not as often as poor minority teens. But what happens next? Affluent white young women, expecting a rewarding and prosperous future, opt for abortions and college. Poor minority young women, appraising their grim prospects, accept early motherhood.[40]

To see the relationship between poverty and early child-bearing, take a quick tour of the Pacific Northwest. Consider Yakima County, Washington: a great sprawling expanse of orchards, migrant labor camps, and Indian reservations stretching east from the Cascade crest. Yakima County has the highest teen birthrate in the entire bioregion. Of every 1,000 women aged fifteen to nineteen in this county, 113 give birth each year. Yakima County is also the poorest county in the bioregion. Of every 1,000 children living there, 301 belong to families that fall below the federal poverty line.[41]

Now go down to Clackamas County, Oregon. Gleaming new Wilsonville High School in the heart of this suburban Portland county brims with sexually active young men and women, just like all the region's secondary schools. But almost no one at Wilsonville High has a baby; the students go to college instead. At 34 per 1,000, the teen birthrate in Clackamas County is less than a third of the rate in Yakima County.[42]

Last tour stop: the North Shore health district of British Columbia, comprising the city of North Vancouver and neighboring jurisdictions across the Lion's Gate Bridge from Vancouver. The North Shore has the bioregion's lowest poverty rate. It also has the lowest rate of teen parenting. At 5 births per 1,000 young women—one-ninth of the region's average (43 per 1,000)—the North Shore makes Sweden (14 per 1,000) look bad.[43]

Statistical analysis confirms the impression of this tour. For the 15 most populous counties, which hold 62 percent of U.S. Northwest population, the child poverty rate predicts the teen birthrate with 83 percent accuracy—in the social sciences, this correlation is astonishingly strong. Every 1 percent increase in the rate of child poverty brings a 3.3 percent increase in the teen birthrate. In B.C., you can tell a health district's teen birthrate with 76 percent accuracy from that district's poverty indicator alone.[44]

Poverty not only causes earlier childbearing, but it also increases the overall birthrate. Fertility declines as income rises. In a 1992 survey of married American women aged thirty to thirty-four, those with poverty incomes (under $10,000) already had 2.3 children each on average and expected to have 2.5 children before they stopped. Middle-class women ($35,000 to $50,000 in family income) had 1.8 children and expected eventually to have 2.2. High-income women (more than $75,000 in family income) had 1.3 children and expected 2.1.[45]

Another study, which investigated educational attainment rather than income (the two are closely correlated), found that college graduates typically have 1.6 to 2.0 children, and often not until their thirties. High school graduates, by contrast, have 2.7 children, often when in their twenties, and those who drop out before high school have 3.2 children.[46]

Obviously, smaller families mean a smaller population, but so does simply delaying births. Consider an imaginary Northwest with a population of 15 million, in which people live 80 years and women have two children each—the first at the age of thirty. If there is no migration, this Northwest has a stable population. Now imagine a single, sudden change: the age of first-time mothers falls abruptly to fifteen years. The younger age of new mothers will double the population to 30 million before restabilizing because six generations will coexist where only three once did.

This illustration is extreme, but it's an extreme worth pondering. Fertility patterns are diverging: the average age of poor first-time mothers is in the low twenties and dropping; the average age of affluent first-time mothers is in the high twenties and rising.

Alleviating poverty not only creates conditions in which women delay childbearing from their teens to their early twenties; it also encourages them to delay births further. Compared with the United States, for example, Canada with its lower poverty rate has lower birthrates among both teens and those twenty to twenty-four.[47]

REPRESENTATIVE MICHAEL CARRELL, an outspoken critic of child support enforcement laws, gets to ask Charlie the last question. "Would you favor a return to the statutory rape laws that we had in the past?"

It's the perfect question, the opening Charlie needs to insert his big idea. Charlie says, "We do have child rape laws in the state of Washington. But I recommend that, rather than just a jail penalty for statutory rape, there be a civil penalty of one-half the cost of raising a child for 18 years." Charlie calls this idea a "judgment at birth": a court-imposed obligation upon the birth of a child. If the adult father of a child born to an unwed school-age mother—or possibly to any unwed mother—does not pay, he has put an indelible stain on his credit history. It's a principle that is both bold and ethical, and it would radically expand the flow of resources to poor mothers, without relying on new taxes.

Later in the day, Charlie explains the concept, which has germinated in the dozens of gatherings of young mothers and their parents that he has organized in recent years. "We're talking about fathers paying half the cost of raising their children. And I don't mean the public-assistance cost; I mean half the cost of raising a child—decent housing, adequate transportation, health care, education through age eighteen, child care—all the things the mothers here today are testifying about. I'd like to see the judgment set at the moderate income level to really lift children out of poverty."

Charlie does not expect this idea to be enacted into law quickly, but he thinks it will gain ground in the long run. "The public assumption is that all these dads are dead-beats, with low incomes and no skills, and they really don't have capacity to support children. We know that isn't true. There are men out there who are ministers and judges and who have fathered children with teen mothers. We know them." But their identity isn't recorded on birth certificates, so the mothers get no financial assistance.

Child support payments, which are poorly collected even from divorced fathers, are virtually nonexistent among unmarried parents who have broken up. Scarcely half of Idaho's single mothers received any child support or alimony payments in 1993, and Idaho was in front of the pack. Of Oregon's single moms, 45 percent got financial help from the fathers of their children; the figure was 37 percent in Montana, 34 percent in Washington, 32 percent in Alaska, and 25 percent in California.[48]

The shares of unwed teenage mothers who receive child support are even lower: in the United States, only 15 percent of never-married teen moms win child support orders, and these lucky few typically receive only $141 a month—one-third of the average promised amount. In Washington State, children are owed $1.7 billion in overdue support payments; poor children are due $1 billion of that.[49]

Welfare reform does include provisions to suspend driver's licenses held by deadbeat dads. But the expected increase in child support payments will mostly go to the state, which subtracts child support payments from its public-assistance grants. Besides, court awards are usually meager. "Here's the existing situation," Charlie says. "You take the guy's income, subtract his expenses, and then, out of what's left over, you decide what should be paid. Most court awards are less than 10 percent of the father's income."

That lets fathers off the hook and abandons their children to need. "If the mother decides not to buy food for the child," Charlie points out, "she's going to be charged with neglect, and she's going to be punished. If the father decides not to buy food for the child, good luck; you gotta catch him. Heck, he doesn't even have to buy food if he's paying 10 percent of his income." A recent study in California found that absent parents are ten times as likely to be current on their car payments as on their child support. What's more, without the establishment of paternity, children are effectively disinherited: their families get no survivor benefits from Social Security or veterans' programs, no pension or life insurance benefits, and no assets. "It's the old bastard clause of the rich," comments Charlie.[50]

A judgment at birth, on the other hand, would make men legally responsible for their offspring, on a par with women. There would be no need for going to court to get a child support award. If fathers weren't bringing up their children themselves, they would automatically be responsible for partially financing the children's upbringing. This scheme would strike deep at the roots of poverty. It would also give men an incentive to attend to contraception more carefully. It would make pregnancy, which is functionally the woman's problem in many relationships, the man's problem, too.

Of course, not every father has the means to lift his children out of poverty. But the principle ought to be enshrined in law, Charlie argues. Exceptions, waivers, and public cost sharing could come later.

And child support ought to be a supplement to, not a substitute for, public assistance because the cure for child poverty is not the kind of welfare reform under consideration in state capitols this year. The cure is a different welfare reform, one transferring more money—much more money—to poor families with children. The quantities of money British Columbia spends, for starters. Or better, the amounts Americans spend on their seniors: America's Social Security system, which redistributes wealth from young, working people to old, retired people has cut senior poverty by two-thirds since 1960.[51]

The difference between welfare for the old and welfare for the young, the public (mis)conceives, is that Social Security and Medicare are retirement plans in which people

take out what they put in. But this is the purest of myths:
typical retirees take out 5 to 20 times what they put in.
The real difference is that welfare for the old pays out
much more money.

Counting the cost of public education, the statistically
average American child receives public assistance worth
about $5,000 a year; the statistically average elder gets about
$15,000. Seniors get universal, publicly supported medical
care; generous monthly income checks indexed to inflation; the once-in-a-lifetime opportunity to cash out of
home ownership tax free; and no requirements that they
sign a "personal responsibility contract" or prove they're
looking for a job. To judge from their actions, North
Americans believe that everyone is entitled to a secure
retirement but not to a secure childhood. (Of course, there's
a political difference between welfare for the old and welfare for the poor, and that difference is decisive: everyone
gets old, or hopes to; not everyone gets poor.)[52]

The possibilities for new forms of support for young
families are ample: childcare centers as part of the public
school system; vastly improved public schools, with one
teacher for, say, each ten children; tax reform to aid working families; universal health care; paid maternity leave; family security stipends for parents with children younger than
five; guaranteed college tuition for every child who can
graduate from high school.

A discredited liberal wish list? Maybe so.

But also a hardheaded, profitable investment strategy.
Middle-aged baby boomers in particular ought to support
it: as seniors, they'll depend directly for their Social Security and Medicare checks on the earnings of today's young.

Without these kinds of investments, how will the system keep supporting the boomers' own retirement? How will the children growing up in poverty today become sufficiently productive to support not only themselves and their children but also their elders?

And only a renewed commitment to targeting child poverty will dramatically slow natural population increase in the Pacific Northwest. Child poverty is the real root of teen births, early childbearing in general, and increased childbearing overall.

THE NEXT DAY, Charlie arrives early and, opening the wrong door, finds himself in hearings on another subject: prisons. Few people are in the hearing room besides some executives from the Department of Corrections—as peculiar an appellation as any in government. This conversation, unlike the welfare reform hearing, is congenial, almost congratulatory. The prison systems' brand-new facilities, and those under construction, are performing admirably, and the committee is pleased. Corrections is a favored department in the legislature.

Because of rising crime—another by-product of poverty—and tougher sentences, Idaho's prison population has nearly tripled since 1985, as has California's. In Montana, Oregon, and Washington, prison population has almost doubled, and Alaska's has grown by half. Only B.C.'s prisons have grown little. The bioregion's total prison population surged 6 percent a year from 1985 to 1995, almost three times the growth of the general population.[53]

This growth has meant a construction boom. Idaho is adding 536 beds to a prison near Boise, and a new 1,250-bed complex is likely to open in the summer of 1999. Oregon is adding 2,332 beds in Malheur County and planning two new 1,636-bed prisons. Washington, having just completed a round of new construction, is drawing plans for a 1,936-bed unit in Grays Harbor County. More than a billion dollars in prison construction is on the books in the Northwest states, and that amount doesn't count operating costs averaging $25,000 a year per inmate.[54]

"Somehow, we can find the money to build and run all these prisons, but we can't find the money to lift children out of poverty," says Charlie. Poverty is expensive: the public pays for it one way or another. Meanwhile, funding for education has been falling relative to the size of the student population. Local school levies increasingly fail across the region. During the 1990s, Washington State has cut real spending per student for K–12 education by 4 percent, for community colleges by 31 percent, and for state colleges and universities by 22 percent. Public postsecondary education is now well beyond the means of the poor.[55]

The second day of welfare reform hearings drags on. In all the testimony, a certain decorum is observed. Suzette Cook is cheerful, sparkly, and upbeat, no matter what anyone says. Committee members show an exaggerated, stylized civility. The people who testify mostly respond with stylized performances of their own. Everyone is sure to say, "Nobody wants to see welfare reform more than I do." Everyone who has ever received public aid, meanwhile, performs an obligatory lament. Over and over again, people say things like "I wanted to contribute to society, but I found myself with two small children and nowhere else to turn." The apparent presumptions are that needing help is shameful, a sign of personal failure, and that raising children does not contribute to society but any paid work does, even if it is operating a deep-fat fryer.

Above all, no one ever speaks in moral terms. No one speaks of injustice. This protocol is standard in North American policy discussions. A minister whose parish includes one of the poorest neighborhoods in New York City's Bronx describes it thus: "Words that are equal to the pain of the poor are pretty easily discredited. A quarter of the truth, stated with lots of indirection, is regarded as more seemly."[56]

But toward the end of the second day, for two embarrassing moments, somebody dares to speak all four quarters of the truth. Maxine Regal from Seattle points out that vastly larger sums are spent on corporate welfare in America—on tax breaks for businesses—and no one is rushing to reform those budget-busting, market-distorting programs. Poor women in America should get substantially more public assistance, not less, she says. This legislation is a crime against women, the poor, minorities, and children. Embarrassment hangs in the room. Even Regal herself appears mildly abashed to be speaking so nakedly about injustice. With well-practiced graciousness, Representative Cook thanks Regal for her testimony.

OLYMPIA, WASHINGTON, April 17, 1997. Washington governor Gary Locke signs legislation ending the entitlement of Washington citizens to cash grants when they are in poverty. Oregon has completed its version of welfare reform, and other Northwest states are also revising their laws. The phrasing Carrie Coppinger Carter objected to, about teenage parenting being destructive to society, does not survive the governor's pen, but the central thrust of the legislation does: "Get a job."

Charlie Langdon begins preparing himself for the repercussions: hundreds of thousands of Northwest children in worsened poverty in the late 1990s and tens of thousands of them pregnant one decade later.

ROOT 2

SEXUAL ABUSE

VANCOUVER, B.C., April 15, 1997. Paige Latin always gets nervous before a talk. Founder of Prostitution Alternatives Counseling and Education (PACE), she has given hundreds of these informal speeches now, but it's still hard to get past the anxiety of standing in front of 20 or 100 people and saying, "Hi. I'm Paige, and I used to be a prostitute." Before she goes into the alternative secondary school where she's speaking today, she smokes a cigarette to calm her nerves. "It's hard sometimes, but talking about it does help the healing," she says. "It washes you of the shame."

That's not why she talks, though. She gives these presentations to find sexual abuse victims, to direct them toward the help they need, and to inoculate others against abuse. "When I'm talking about what it feels like to be sexually abused, I see this look in their eyes—the kids who are being abused—of 'Oh, my God! That's what's been happening to me.' There are three or four in every class."

These three or four are at risk of involvement in prostitution; the two-thirds of them who are females are at even greater risk of early and repeated childbearing. Victims of abuse often feel that having a baby will help them heal from the violation they have suffered.[57]

Inside the classroom, the students clamber into chairs and onto desktops, and a counselor introduces Paige. At first, the fifteen- and sixteen-year-olds look at her as if she were a freak. She launches into her story.

It's an excruciating tale. It turns the stomach and incites rage, and Paige seems to live it over as she speaks, her slender form bent almost double. "Three-fourths to 95 percent of us—women who have been involved in prostitution—are survivors of childhood sexual abuse." She leans toward them, her dark eyes darting about the room, checking in with every other pair of eyes. Her voice has the kind of expressive lilt that would have taken her far on the radio, but she uses it, along with every other gift she has, to attack prostitution. The students are reserved, but they are listening.[58]

"Personally, I remember being sexually abused from age two," Paige recounts. "My parents didn't know about it, and I didn't know anything different. I thought it happened to everyone. I was abused again at age three by a guy that used to work for my dad."

Like most sexually abused children, Paige came from a family with more than its share of problems. Her mother suffered untreated clinical depression. Her father traveled extensively in his struggling construction business, and his income left them far short of middle class. The pressure cooker of poverty creates the conditions in which most abuse occurs—economic and physical insecurity, dysfunctional families, emotional disorders, substance abuse, and hopelessness. In the United States, children from poor families (incomes below $15,000) are 18 times as likely to be sexually abused and more than 20 times as likely to be seriously injured by physical abuse as children from families with incomes above $30,000.[59]

Most of the students are leaning in toward Paige now, regarding her as less of a circus sideshow. "At age five," Paige recalls, "it was a guy at a gas station. He gave me hepatitis, and I almost died. Ages six to eight, it was the guy that ran the tourist info booth next to the playground. He penetrated me at age six."

Abuse seemed to seek her out—an uncannily commonplace pattern among abuse victims. Sexual abuse is a curse. It truncates normal development of the ability to sense unsafe situations and untrustworthy people. It corrodes children's self-esteem, making them desperate for approval, affection, and safety and teaching them to expect violation as the price of these commodities. Abuse also causes learning difficulties, attention disorders, and physical and cognitive dysfunctions. These disorders, in turn, can compound victims' self-loathing; they may come to believe what their abusers tell them about being sexual objects. They can become conditioned to submit to abuse and, if the abuse is long-lasting, they may become accustomed to trading sex for security or other needs.[60]

"Another guy abused me from age eight to twelve," says Paige. The class is wide-eyed. "That's the one that affected me the most. It was my girlfriend's dad." Authority figures commit more than half of all rapes. "He would give me alcohol and cigarettes and money," she says. "That's where I think I got my introduction into prostitution. He did a real number on my head, saying that I was 'really good at this,' that kind of stuff." He coerced her into sexual intercourse, she estimates, about once a week for four years.[61]

All eyes are on Paige—almost. A boy in the back of the room is now avoiding her glance. He pulls the hood of his sweatshirt up, drops his chin, and begins furiously doodling on his desk. Paige watches him for a moment, then puts her head in her hand and squeezes her eyes together. He is an abuse survivor, she is convinced. No one guesses why she has paused. She takes a breath and goes on.

At thirteen, she was brutally raped by a stranger who abducted her at gunpoint from her family's motel room while they were on vacation in Florida. More than 60 percent of rape victims are under eighteen. Approximately 1 American woman in 1,000 reports suffering a rape each year; Canadian women report rapes at one-fifth that rate.[62]

Later, a police officer asked her, "Where did he rape you?" She says it was the first time she understood what she had experienced. "The word reverberated in my head, 'He *raped* me! That's what's been happening to me my whole life? *Rape?*'"

In the months that followed, she suffered a full-scale psychological crisis with nowhere to turn. To escape the flashbacks, anxiety attacks, and nightmares, she medicated herself. She had already abused drugs. "I started drinking when I was six. I started sniffing glue when I was nine." But after the rape, she took to drugs with a vengeance. "At times, I tried to kill myself by overdosing." Over the next 15 years, she used alcohol, speed, marijuana, powder and crack cocaine, heroin, and every imaginable kind of pill.

On the other side of the room, another boy has withdrawn into himself. She makes a mental note. She's not as sure about him as the boy who is doodling, but she is suspicious. And she's getting an uneasy feeling about two girls sitting on a bookcase against the wall. Their eyes are too big; they look like abuse survivors, too.

When she was fifteen, she left her home in the small Rocky Mountain town of Williams Lake, B.C. "I moved to Toronto," she says, "and it didn't take me very long to end up out on the streets. I worked as a prostitute from age fifteen on and off, mostly on, until I was twenty-nine. I'm thirty-five now."

Paige Latin has done this same basic presentation at dozens of schools, youth detention centers, universities, hospitals, and civic group meetings across B.C. in recent years. As far as she knows, she and a few other former prostitutes she has recruited are the only people speaking out about sexual abuse to B.C.'s young people and the professionals who work with them. She continues her story, telling how she got out of prostitution, thanks to a former prostitute who counseled her by phone for months.

In 1994, Paige established the nonprofit charitable group PACE to help women escape from—and avoid getting into—prostitution. Over time, she has focused more of her energy on preventing the sexual abuse from which prostitution stems. She would speak to young people full time if she could, but PACE has little money, and priorities are numerous. Paige herself is living on unemployment insurance as she makes the rounds of Rotary Club luncheons, raising funds for an emergency shelter for women trying to get off the streets.

"If abuse is happening in your life, you can talk to Natasha," Paige tells the class, pointing to the counselor. "Natasha can help you to get to a counseling service that will meet you wherever you want. Or if it's happening to a friend. Nobody ever talked with me about sexual abuse when I was a kid, and I don't want that to happen to you."

Later, she will call Natasha about the four she has identified. She has a knack for finding abuse victims. She says, "The terrible thing is, my hunches are almost always right." Child abuse and neglect reports have risen in the Northwest in recent years—by 80 percent in Washington in the past decade—in step with a rise in youth poverty. But many of these reports are not investigated. Nationwide in the United States, overstretched child protection authorities investigated fewer than 30 percent of reported abuse cases. And experts believe that most abuse is never reported at all.[63]

PAIGE DOESN'T TALK MUCH about the other major consequence of child sexual abuse: teen parenting. But it's a consequence far more common than prostitution, so her fight against abuse is also preventing teen births. Sixty-two percent of school-age mothers are victims of sexual abuse before becoming pregnant—at least twice and more likely five times as large a proportion as among the general population of teenage girls.[64]

The litany of abuses they have suffered is shocking. Forty-three percent of school-age mothers are rape victims; 5 percent of them conceived their first child by rape. Physical abuse is also rampant: 59 percent have been hit with a belt or strap, 31 percent have been hit with a stick, 26 percent have been thrown against a wall, 5 percent have been intentionally burned or scalded, and 22 percent have been beaten up by a man to the point of requiring medical treatment. (In ASAP's lobbying on welfare reform, it has vehemently objected to proposals that teen mothers should be required to live in their parents' home. The problem all too often *is* their parents' home.)[65]

The statistically average school-age mother in the Northwest is a white, poor, socially isolated sixteen-year-old high school dropout who lives at a parent's home in a working-class neighborhood. Beginning just before her tenth birthday, she was molested repeatedly by a twenty-seven-year-old family member, most likely her stepfather. At age thirteen, she was raped by a twenty-three-year-old acquaintance, and she was later raped twice more by other older men.[66]

Deeply wounded by abuse, she began voluntary sex—if you can call it that—without contraception at fourteen. Her partner was nineteen; he promised her love and protection from her abusers, but he sometimes hit her and coerced her into having sex. She changed partners frequently and, with another nineteen-year-old man, became pregnant shortly before her sixteenth birthday. Because of the abuse, she is more likely to suffer depression, anxiety, suicidal feelings, drug and alcohol addiction, low self-esteem, further abuse and coercive sex, and infection with sexually transmitted diseases. As a victim, she is also at increased risk of abusing her own children, exposing them to others who may abuse them, and losing custody of her children to child-welfare authorities.[67]

The statistically average school-age mom is also at very high risk of having additional children. One-fourth of sexually abused girls who become mothers in high school have given birth two or more times before their twenty-third birthdays, and one-third of all births to teenage mothers

are actually second births. This pattern may persist because young women beaten down by poverty and taught
at an early age to submit to repeated sexual violation often
look on reproduction as a healing event. Early childbearing is part of the pathology of child abuse, but to the victim, it appears to be part of the cure.[68]

Paige Latin fits this profile almost perfectly—except she's
not a mother, and only because of an inherited health con-
dition that makes it difficult for her to carry a baby to term.
Tragically, she's had five miscarriages and fervently hopes
medical treatment will allow her to have a child soon.

What's needed, Paige believes, is public mobilization
against abuse of children by adults. Abuse doesn't appear
on the radar screens of most official agencies. Even the
gatherers of official health statistics ignore child abuse: "In
1995," writes Mike Males in his book *Scapegoat Generation,*
"a spokeswoman for the National Commission on Child
Abuse complained that it was easier to get information
from the Centers for Disease Control on soccer goalpost
injuries than on the epidemic of adult violence against
children."[69]

"Teachers should all be trained in recognizing sexual
abuse symptoms," argues Paige, "and every school should
have a trained sexual abuse counselor. There should be
free sexual abuse counseling available for all ages." The
sole provider of low-cost sexual abuse counseling in British Columbia closed its waiting list seven months ago, Paige
says, and it was a year long then. Doctors, nurses, police
officers, medical assistants, and judges are not properly
trained either, she maintains, so victims of abuse are too
often traumatized as they seek help. The investigation of

reported child abuse needs dramatic expansion, abuse victims need safe havens in every community, and hundreds
of people like Paige should be wandering the Northwest
telling their stories to catalyze change.

As things stand now, most adults do not know the signs
of abuse, are uncomfortable discussing it, and do not know
what to do when they suspect it. Meanwhile, six-year-olds
have a better chance of knowing what to do if a stranger
offers them candy than if their uncle tries to rape them.
Statistically, sexual assault by a parent or parent-substitute
in the home is 200 times more common than abduction
off the streets by a stranger. The Northwest lives in a massive state of denial about the sexual crimes suffered by its
children, and an added increment of population growth is
only one of the consequences.[70]

ROOT 3

─────────

INADEQUATE FAMILY-
PLANNING SERVICES

AN ESTIMATED 10 percent of babies born in the
Northwest are unwanted at conception—they are conceived accidentally at a time when the mother wants no
more children. Another 26 percent of Northwest births
result from pregnancies that the mother regards as wrongly
timed. These births—many of them to teens—usually
happen one to three years earlier than desired.[71]

Here lies another root of population growth—insuffi-
cient access to reproductive health care, including family
planning and safe, legal abortion services. Earlier childbearing, even when the difference is only a few years,
increases population slightly over the long run, so better
contraception can make a difference.

Unintended pregnancy happens to all kinds of women,
but it is especially common among women who are poor,
young, single, or all three. It is common among the poor
because many poor women have little motivation to avoid
pregnancy. Parenting is one of the more rewarding opportunities available to them, so contraception is less of a priority. It is common among the young and single because
these women are more likely to be in shorter-term relationships. A disproportionate share of unintended pregnancies

occur in the unstable beginning or on-and-off ending of a relationship. At these times, commitments are in flux, emotions are inflamed, communications are complicated, and many couples do not use contraception. Young women and single women spend more of their time in these transitional phases than do older or married women.[72]

The share of births from unintended pregnancies has been climbing. Nationwide in the United States—and the Northwest states appear to conform with the norm—the unintended share of births rose from 37 percent in 1982 to 44 percent in 1990. Yet unintended pregnancies need not be so common. Canadian women surveyed in the mid-1980s reported 40 percent fewer unintended pregnancies than their American counterparts, and Dutch women reported fewer than half as many as did Canadians.[73]

Unintended pregnancies *can* be prevented through public action. Access to affordable reproductive health care services reduces the birthrate. Specifically, statistical tests across all 50 American states show that access to local family-planning and abortion clinics, to Medicaid coverage of family-planning and abortion services, and to nearby obstetrician-gynecologists all reduce the birthrate. Access to abortion services is especially important: as distance to an abortion provider increases, abortion rates measurably decline; one-third of American women live in counties that lack any identifiable abortion provider.[74]

U.S. government-supported family-planning programs have been quite successful. A review of scholarly literature by the National Academy of Sciences' Institute of Medicine in Washington, D.C., concluded that both government-funded family-planning clinics and Medicaid-funded

contraceptive services do help reduce unintended births
and a long list of reproductive health ailments. Federal support for family-planning clinics in Washington State, for
example, prevented an estimated 48,000 unintended pregnancies in 1991 alone.[75]

Instituted in the 1960s and 1970s, federal family-
planning programs have turned family planning from a
privilege of those who can afford a private doctor into a
right for everyone, including the young, the single, and the
poor. Unwanted births among poor married women have
plunged, just as they did decades earlier among married
women who were not poor. The public apparently recog-
nizes the benefit of these programs: 72 percent of citizens
in the United States endorse government provision of contraceptive services to all who need them.[76]

Sadly, political winds have blown the other direction,
and funding for family planning and other reproductive
health programs has dwindled. From 1980 to 1992, federal
family-planning outlays, adjusted for inflation, declined by
more than 70 percent. In 1994, federal funds transferred to
the Northwest states for family planning averaged only
$2.03 per resident, and the states didn't add much. Califor-
nia allocated $2.73 per citizen that year. Washington spent
$1.56; Alaska, 83 cents; Oregon, about 74 cents; Montana
gambled nothing more than a threepenny ante; and Idaho—
with the highest birthrate in the Northwest—spent abso-
lutely nothing. B.C.'s more generous funding went through
the national health care system and couldn't be tracked.[77]

The cuts hurt. In Washington State, government-
supported family-planning clinics now have funding to
serve scarcely 45 percent of eligible women. Little public

money goes to support research into new contraceptive techniques, even though efforts to improve contraceptive methods have come to a virtual standstill. Only four companies remain involved in contraceptive research, down from a dozen in the early 1980s.[78]

Neither is there much public money to raise awareness of little-used but effective emergency methods. The so-called morning-after pill, long known to researchers, remains unknown to most women. Yet it's not a new pill at all but simply a technique of taking a double or triple dose of certain common birth control pills a day or two after unprotected intercourse. It is highly effective and has few side effects. Fearful of abortion politics, however, no pharmaceutical company is packaging and marketing birth control pills for this emergency use; indeed, none has even applied for approval from the U.S. Food and Drug Administration. The FDA, to its credit, took the unprecedented step of approving the pills and issuing detailed instructions on dosages and timing so that women could use the method on their own.[79]

B.C.'s universal health care system guarantees comprehensive contraceptive coverage for all, but elsewhere in the Northwest, millions of people have medical insurance that pays for childbirth but not for contraception. This penny-wise, pound-foolish approach to reproductive health puts highly effective methods such as hormonal implants out of reach for those who cannot afford the up-front cost. Almost all health insurers would save money by covering all forms of contraception, yet just 20 percent of health plans in Washington State do so. Another 7 percent cover only birth control pills. The remaining 73 percent of health insurers in Washington do not cover any form of contraception, and Washington is typical of American states in this regard. Yet the cost to an insurer of a single delivery would pay for 15 years of contraceptives.[80]

Safeguarding women's right to choose abortion is also a priority. An excruciating moral decision for any woman and her loved ones, abortion remains, from a public health perspective, an indispensable medical procedure. Without access to safe, legal abortions, women would again begin to die from botched illegal abortions as they did in the United States before the procedure was legalized nationwide in 1973.

A Northwest that aspires to lead the world in slowing population growth would aim to guarantee universal access to reproductive health services. If all pregnancies were intentional, the long-term rate of population growth from all sources would decline by about 12 percent.[81]

ROOT 4

SUBSIDIES TO DOMESTIC MIGRATION

SALEM, OREGON, April 30, 1997. State Representative Chuck Carpenter is one rock-ribbed conservative who's had his fill of population growth. His legislative district on the west edge of greater Portland was flooding with newcomers even before he won office in the 1994 Republican revolution. Migrants have trekked to Portland from California and points east across the United States, drawn by a white-hot job market and the lure of a city among the most livable in North America. "I probably have one of the fastest-growing districts in the state," says Chuck. "I'm right on the edge of all the high-tech growth in what we call the Silicon Forest. It is growing phenomenally fast."

Accommodating these migrants, however, has been expensive for the communities where they have landed, both in environmental degradation and in dollars and cents. The burden on longtime taxpayers particularly offends Chuck's sense of fairness. "My constituents—some of them have been here 30 or 40 years—are increasingly paying for the additional schools and infrastructure." So, as their chosen advocate in state government, Chuck is out to stop subsidizing outlanders' moving into his Willamette Valley homeland.

With the support of the land use-planning advocates 1000 Friends of Oregon, Chuck Carpenter introduced House Bill 3070 to the legislature in Salem. The bill would require local governments to show taxpayers the bottom line every time those governments proposed opening a new tract of rural land for development. It's a bold new idea—one.that may well catch on elsewhere as the costs of providing infrastructure for newcomers mount. Unfortunately, this bill has a long way to go in Salem. Chuck explains, "I'm a member of the majority party, and this is one issue I disagree with my Republican colleagues on." In the end, however, Chuck is sure he will prevail: "My conservative roots tell me that this bill should be a conservative issue."

The ironies of this case are piled deep. First, there's the politics: a free marketeer teaming up with planning advocates to protect local taxpayers. Then there's the fact that Chuck himself is a prototypical Northwest migrant. Raised and educated in the East, he came to Portland to take a job at one of the Northwest's booming companies—Nike. Roughly half of northwesterners are first-generation residents born elsewhere, and more people come to the Northwest to take a job than for any other reason.[82]

OREGON'S WILLAMETTE VALLEY stretching south from Portland is the destination of most migrants to Oregon, just as it was for nineteenth-century pioneers following the Oregon Trail. But virtually every hill and dale in the Pacific Northwest is on the receiving end of population movements. Domestic migration has accounted for 46 percent of regional growth since 1980, bringing 1.5

million people. And most of them—unlike most immigrants from abroad and unlike the region's newborn babies—are full-fledged North American consumers. They tend to be well educated and to command incomes larger than the regional norm, which usually means they also leave larger-than-average footprints on the environment: more cars, bigger houses, more waste.[83]

Long-distance moves are part and parcel of the larger, and distinctly North American, phenomenon of raging mobility. The United States and Canada have some of the highest internal relocation rates in the world. Every year, one American in six moves to a new county or state, and Canadians move almost as much. Every five years, one-fourth of the population in average American counties trades places with people from other counties. This rootlessness is the largest reason that North American places lack the sense of community taken for granted in settlements on other continents.[84]

High mobility is credited by some demographers and economists with enhancing individual liberty, broadening employment options, and releasing the supposedly stultifying grip of family ties. But it is also associated with higher crime and higher divorce rates, with widening economic inequality, and with dissipation of the social ties that bind individuals into societies.[85]

Still, North Americans are increasingly putting down roots. Nationwide statistics show mobility decreasing among Americans and Canadians. Only 2.6 percent of Americans moved to another state in 1993, the lowest figure since midcentury. In Canada, where one has to move much farther to reach another province, almost 2 percent of the population moved to a different province in 1973; in 1993, fewer than 1 percent did. These changes have partly resulted from aging of the population. Moving is concentrated among people in their twenties and diminishes at older ages as people settle down.[86]

Subsiding wanderlust has yet to translate into smaller numbers of newcomers in the Pacific Northwest, however. The region has been drawing increasing shares of all movers. In 1994, for example, British Columbia gained population from every other Canadian province. And the Northwest states are among the fastest growing in America.[87]

Yet despite the sheer volume of arriving migrants, a remedial public goal—simply slowing migration—is not adequate. Rather, the Northwest should focus its energies on the higher goal of nurturing communities—communities that hold their residents together; communities in which families invest their time, energy, and money; communities in which people choose to spend their lives.

People stay and move for similar reasons—all related to the overall quality of life in a given locale—such as economic opportunities, proximity to family, access to natural and cultural amenities, and sense of community. Communities that retain their residents have much in common, including strong job markets, lots of homeowners, older-than-average residents, and high percentages of families with children. Stable communities also have more than their share of locally owned manufacturing and retail businesses, community associations and nonprofit groups, churches and churchgoers. They also have fewer class divisions: income distribution in low-mobility settlements is more equitable than in average-mobility settlements. In short, places where people stay are places full of citizens who are personally invested and engaged in the places where they live.[88]

Policymaking focused on retaining longtime residents will serve communities' own immediate interests; it will also lead to the only viable policy options for slowing migration—eliminating biases that favor newcomers at the expense of current residents. What else could Northwest jurisdictions do? Put up roadblocks? Impose entry fees on newcomers? Basic legal principles in both Canada and the United States—not to mention ethical ones—protect the right to relocate domestically and the right to equal treatment with other citizens. So the Northwest cannot directly control domestic migration; it can affect mobility only indirectly—for example, by no longer subsidizing associated activities like real estate development.[89]

IF YOU WANT TO SEE where Chuck Carpenter's bill would first sink its heels into Willamette Valley soil, go out to where, in local parlance, "the TV hits the UGB." Travel along the Tualatin Valley Highway ("the TV") west from Beaverton, past miles of relentless strip development, until you reach Southwest 209th Avenue. There, just after you pass the quarter-mile-long frontage of an Intel computer chip plant, the highway briefly skirts Portland's urban growth boundary (UGB)—the legal edge of urbanization around Portland under Oregon's trendsetting growth-management law—and development abruptly stops. On your left unfolds a 500-acre tract of prime farmland, some of the most fertile in Washington County. Nearby a sign proclaims, "Llamas for sale." The country does not last long, however. The UGB peels off from the Tualatin Valley Highway, and roadside development resumes on both sides as you approach Hillsboro.[90]

This almost treeless tract of farm, says Mary Webber, an official of greater Portland's Metro Council, "is a developer's dream—just one big hunk of land." Already, a sprawling new maze of single-family houses nears completion behind the Intel facility, and if the Genstar Land Company has its way, the same thing will happen on the farm where the TV hits the UGB. Genstar has bought an option on the land from the Sisters of Saint Mary, an order of Catholic nuns that owns a convent nearby and a title deed for this farm, donated by a devout supporter. If the UGB is rolled back, Genstar can put in cookie-cutter houses marching to the horizon. That's the kind of development Chuck Carpenter worries about: housing built on this land, even if it turns a profit for the developer, would turn a loss for Washington County.[91]

"What we're saying here is that taxpayers should know the true costs of expanding the urban growth boundary," Chuck says. Each new house requires more urban infrastructure: schools; roads; water pipes; sewer and drainage systems; and police, fire, and ambulance services. To pay for these public services, many jurisdictions have begun charging builders fees called systems development charges.

Nowhere, however, do the development charges fully reimburse local treasuries for the expenses of development. In Oregon, fees levied against the builder of a typical new three-bedroom single-family home, like those commonly sold to newcomers, range from $1,000 to $6,500. Yet according to Eugene-based planning consultant Eben Fodor, the full cost of providing infrastructure for those newcomers is $24,500. Local taxpayers get saddled with the difference—a difference that adds up to between $300 million and $600 million a year statewide.[92]

For now, the urban growth boundary protects the farm beside the TV Highway from treasury-draining development, but the boundary is not immovable. It's less a fixed town wall than a 20-year supply of land. Based on population projections, UGB planners in government are supposed to allot enough land to accommodate 20 years of growth. They're also supposed to designate another 30-year supply of land in several categories of reserves. Then, if population growth necessitates moving the UGB, it jumps to the edge of the first tier of reserves. Near the TV Highway, it would move from the edge of the road to the other side of the Sisters' farm.[93]

The possibility is real, says Chuck: "There's been a plan afoot to expand the urban growth boundary" because of the onslaught of migration into the Willamette Valley. Under H.B. 3070, however, government would have to calculate the impact on taxpayers before the UGB could jump the field—calculate what it would cost to build the schools, sewer lines, and roads that would be needed if 2,500 human beings, rather than acres of crops, were planted beside the Tualatin Valley Highway. Under H.B. 3070, any change in the UGB would trigger a taxpayer impact statement, and taxpayer impact statements might fuel a ground swell of demand for higher fees on new development. Higher fees, in turn, would make moving to new developments in

the Willamette Valley more expensive and thus, Chuck
hopes, discourage migration.

ANOTHER SUBSIDY FROM POORER residents to
richer newcomers is government-sponsored industrial recruitment. One of the Northwest's largest taxpayer-funded
programs for luring factories is Oregon's Strategic Investments Program (SIP), which exempts most of the assessed
value of new factories in the high-tech industries from
property taxes. Since 1993, five firms have qualified for
SIP by committing to build plants that manufacture computer chips and other hardware for the information age.
These plants, which will have a combined value of more
than $9 billion when completed, are each taxed on only
the first $100 million of assessed value—a tax break that
will cost local and state governments more than $17 mil-
lion annually for 15 years. Current residents and businesses—
most of which are smaller and poorer than the multina-
tional corporations enrolled in the program—make up the
difference, either in higher taxes or in lower-quality public
services. Washington State, too, has granted millions of dollars in sales tax exemptions to new manufacturers.[94]
 Both states hope that the jobs new companies bring
will go to native residents, but many jobs do not. Short-
ages of skilled labor push many high-tech companies
to recruit out-of-state workers. The Oregon Economic
Development Commission estimates that the five SIP semi-
conductor plants—which have accounted for perhaps one-
twentieth of the state's job growth since 1993—could bring
a total population increase of 26,000 people by 2012.[95]

Ending tax breaks for industrial recruitment and charging full price for residential development would slow migration into the Northwest, but no one can say by how much. The effect might be very big or very small. To date, specialists have not been able to determine the numerical importance of the various factors influencing mobility, such as job markets, housing markets, cultural offerings, and natural beauty. So the relative impact of subsidies on mobility—as opposed to their impact on fairness—is unknown.[96]

The conventional wisdom about domestic migration holds that businesses locate their facilities based purely on bottom-line considerations, such as proximity to markets and costs of labor. These decisions supposedly determine the geographic distribution of jobs, and people relocate accordingly. Profit, tracked hourly in the fluttering of stock prices, thus puts people in their places. This view is a misconception—and a dangerous generalization. Some migration does work more or less according to this description, but it's probably less than half the total.[97]

The central truth about mobility is that migrants move to places where they believe their lives will be better. Jobs count in the equation, but so do family, friends, safety, community, beauty, environmental quality, and all the things that contribute to quality of life. People choose places and then go looking for work as often as they choose work and then passively accept the places that work sends them. And businesses situate themselves for the same reasons: they set up shop in places they perceive to be good places to set up shop. "We want to grow where smart people want to live," says John Young, chairman of Hewlett-Packard, which operates large plants in the Willamette Valley and other parts of the Pacific Northwest.[98]

The relative livability of the Northwest has drawn migrants as much as has its steaming job market, and livability has also heated up the job market by keeping businesses here and attracting new ones. Since the mid-1980s, the Northwest states have dramatically outperformed the rest of the United States in almost all economic measures. In recent years, Idaho, once regularly tormented by sluggish economic growth, grew at more than three times the national average in employment, income, and earnings; in these same terms, Washington and Oregon have grown at more than twice the national rate.[99]

So eliminating subsidies that benefit migrants will slow job-pulled mobility, but it may not slow the migration drawn by the Northwest's attractive environment and lively communities. And how this balance works out cannot be predicted.

BACK ON THE Tualatin Valley Highway, telephone poles double as bus stops. A surprising number of people wait beside them, just a few feet from the roaring traffic. A brightly painted Tri-Met bus drives by, sporting a bumper sticker that says, "219 cars are at home because I'm on the road." Judging by the number of people on board wearing the uniforms of low-wage service jobs, you might guess that many of those 219 cars do not exist.

The taxpayer impact statement that Representative Carpenter proposes would arm the men and women on the bus with full disclosure about the consequences of population growth. At a minimum, they'd know that new-comers don't pay their way, and residents might demand higher development fees. Higher fees could mean lower general taxes or better public services, either of which would help strengthen existing communities. If new developments paid for themselves, settled lower-income people would no longer be subsidizing mobile higher-income people. The people on the bus wouldn't be subsidizing the people in the cars that trap the bus in traffic jams.

Unfortunately, a mountain of other legislation will receive attention before House Bill 3070; the bill is unlikely to make it out of committee this session. Chuck Carpenter is not naive about its chances: "We're going to have a lot of difficulty," he admits, but he's quietly confident, too. "When you look at this bill on its merit, it's a very conservative idea. My definition of *conservative* is that you're concerned about the burden that you put on taxpayers."

ROOT 5

MISGUIDED
IMMIGRATION LAWS

IMMIGRATION BOOSTS the Northwest's population substantially. Since 1980, almost 400,000 international immigrants have moved to the region, accounting for 12 percent of growth.[100] Yet slowing this flow poses tremendous ethical quandaries. Indeed, encouraging ample immigration makes intuitive sense if you support immigrants' struggles and believe that the cultural mosaic of past immigrants lends vibrancy to North American life. Besides, closing the door to poorer newcomers seems unjust. But closer study reveals misconceptions at the heart of this view, too.

Of course, historically, northwesterners are all immigrants to one degree or another. Some have just arrived—walking down the jetway of a 747 from Hong Kong at the Vancouver, B.C., airport or hitchhiking up the coast from Mexico. Others have been in the Northwest for generations, descended from immigrants who came across the Bering Strait on foot 10,000 years ago; or from European farmers who crossed the continent on the early rail lines, seeking a dryland homestead in the Palouse; or from Asian laborers who steamed across the Pacific, hungry for any kind of employment that didn't ban them through racist labor laws; or from African Americans, brought to the New

World in shackles and drawn to the Northwest by good jobs and a more liberal public; or from southeast Asian refugees scattered to the four winds by warfare. Canada and the United States have long welcomed newcomers from abroad. Comprising just one-twentieth of world population, these two countries are home to one-fifth of the world's living international migrants—people who reside in a country other than the one where they were born. The Pacific Northwest is populated by every lineage, ethnicity, race, creed, nationality, and linguistic branch of the human tree. And all of them are north-westerners, equally deserving of respect and treatment in accordance with their rights.[101]

But supporting recent immigrants is not the same as supporting open-throttle immigration. The United States and Canada are among fewer than a dozen countries that allow immigration at all, and, as two of the richest nations in the world, they confront a virtually limitless pool of potential immigrants. The question is not whether to limit immigration but how much to limit it and—even more important—on what criteria to base the decision.

History is no guide. In the 1980s and 1990s, Canada and the United States opened the doors to immigration wider than at almost any time during this century, but the two nations have alternately opened and closed those doors throughout their histories. They have sometimes done so for good reasons, sometimes for bad, but rarely have their policies reflected any kind of public consensus about immigration's place in their societies.

Both north and south of the forty-ninth parallel, immigration debaters generally phrase their arguments in

terms of national interest, usually defined narrowly in terms
of economic growth, though they sometimes invoke other
considerations. Globalist liberals, mindful of the gaping disparities in world income and conscious of the racism that
motivates some anti-immigration sentiment, favor generous admission levels. Old-school liberals, concerned about
the effects of immigration on the working class, support
restrictions.

Meanwhile, the right divides between economic and
cultural conservatives. The former, including big business
interests, favor open immigration as a way to expand markets and labor supply. The latter would restrict immigration to protect the stability of national culture and values.
In the United States, recent immigrants and business tend
to lobby for high immigration quotas, and trade unions
and cultural conservatives tend to support low quotas.

Rarely in this debate is careful consideration given to
what's best for the world's poor—both those in developing
countries and those in industrial countries. Yet alleviating
poverty in both places is a primary global challenge and
the key to slowing global population growth. Just as poverty in the Northwest is the primary cause of high birthrates, extreme poverty in developing countries has led to
the rapid growth there. To make headway in either immigration policy, population policy, or policies to help the
poor, alternatives ought to be judged primarily from their
impacts on equity—the linchpin in all these issues.

Rapid immigration corrodes the prospects of the poor
because most immigrants, though poor compared with
North Americans, are highly productive members of their
societies. High immigration augments economic growth

in North America but reduces economic growth in immigrants' home countries, and most of those countries need such growth far more than North America does. Immigrants to the United States and Canada tend to be better educated, younger, and more enterprising than their stay-at-home peers. Much immigration into North America represents a brain drain from other parts of the world.[102]

In addition, immigration depresses wages for the poorest North Americans—especially recent immigrants—by creating competition for less-skilled labor. Writes Harvard political scientist George Borjas, "Current immigration redistributes wealth from unskilled workers, whose wages are lowered by immigrants, to skilled workers and owners of companies that buy immigrants' services."[103]

Canada admits more immigrants, relative to its population, than the United States because of its historical links to the British Commonwealth, and British Columbia becomes home to many of them. The province was second only to Ontario as a destination for newcomers to Canada in 1992, and Vancouver alone absorbed 12 percent of these newcomers. Some 22 percent of B.C.'s population was born outside Canada.[104]

In the Northwest states, only 6 percent of the population was born in a foreign land, although the figure is slowly rising. The Northwest states are not a major destination of immigrants; 70 percent of U.S. immigrants go to California, Texas, and four other port-of-entry states.[105]

Still, immigration to other states speeds the Northwest's growth by chain reaction. California is both the single largest destination of immigrants to the United States and, not surprisingly, the single largest source of domestic migrants to the Pacific Northwest. Immigrants create competition for less-skilled jobs, pushing wages down and prompting some low-income native-born residents to seek employment elsewhere. As international migrants congregate in a few of what demographers call "immigrant magnet" cities such as Los Angeles, native-born residents of these cities—especially those without college degrees—are increasingly squeezed out of the job market. They, in turn, move to "native magnet" cities, such as Portland, Seattle, and Boise.[106]

Over most of this century, domestic migrants to Washington State have been highly educated and affluent, but by the second half of the eighties and the early nineties, the balance had shifted toward poorer migrants, many of them from California.[107]

Most immigrants to both Canada and the United States are admitted in three official categories: family reunification, employment visas, and refugees. Family reunification is the largest category in both countries, although Canada plans to boost admissions for employment above those to reunite families. Between 1992 and 1994, 44 percent of legal immigrants to Canada were admitted for family reasons, 43 percent entered as employment immigrants, and about 15 percent were refugees. During the same years, the United States admitted more family immigrants (58 percent), fewer employment immigrants (15 percent), and the same share of refugees.[108]

Families, jobs, and refugee protection are laudable reasons for keeping the immigration doors open. In practice, however, many citizens would be disheartened to learn how far the reality of immigration policy diverges from the ideals symbolized by the Statue of Liberty and the Maple

Leaf. Ensuring that victims of human rights abuses have safe havens is a sacred obligation of any free nation, but many people admitted as refugees bear little resemblance to the desperately persecuted castaways the term evokes.

Likewise, family reunification does not only allow citizens who marry abroad to bring their spouses and young children home with them. It also allows them to bring their spouses' adult brothers and sisters. These siblings can later bring their spouses and children, and so on. Compared with other categories of immigration, family reunification tends to extend entry to workers with fewer skills. And despite assurances to the contrary from its proponents, economics most definitely motivates some immigration that reunites families. Logically, a family can be reunited in either spouse's home country, yet family reunification moves several times as many people into North America as out of it.[109]

Finally, employment immigration, which allows entry on the basis of employment skills, welcomes well-educated people from less-developed countries to North America. Many of them come originally to study in universities but never take their new knowledge back home. Three-fourths of foreign medical students in the United States remain there, in effect doing a real disservice to their home countries. This trend aids and abets the brain drain, among the least noted and most serious obstacles to lasting development in less-industrialized countries. Many of the Third World's best and brightest—potential civic leaders, educators, and entrepreneurs—live in North American cities, their work further enriching an already affluent continent.[110]

Most family immigrants to North America are not highly skilled, and they compete for employment with native-born workers. Workers in 47 major Canadian industries are losing jobs or wages because of high immigration rates, and immigration is responsible for about 44 percent of the decline in wages for high school dropouts in the United States since 1980.[111]

Ultimately, a cheap, malleable labor force with fewer legal rights strengthens corporate managers against native-born laborers, and huge corporate interests lobby aggressively for ample immigration quotas, including family immigration. In an era when yawning chasms have opened between rich and poor in North America as well as globally, open immigration exacerbates inequality both on this continent and between North America and other nations.

Illegal immigration is thought by many to be the largest part of immigration, but it accounts for only one-fourth of all immigrants in the United States and for a much smaller share in Canada. In the Northwest states, illegal immigration is much less common than the public believes. Approximately 85 percent of illegal immigrants in the United States live in six port-of-entry states, none of which is in the Northwest. Still, probably tens of thousands of illegal immigrants do live in the region. The narrow challenge is to slow illegal immigration without violating the civil rights of legal immigrants who might be falsely accused. The broader challenge—as with all immigration— is to strive toward a global future with fewer disparities in living standards. In a sustainable world, there would not be tens of millions of people who felt compelled to travel to faraway places in search of economic security.[112]

A real immigration reform—one based on the criterion of aiding the poor—would safeguard politically oppressed refugees, allow for true but limited family re-unification, and scrutinize employment visa applications to slow the brain drain. It would end up closing the immigration door quite a bit—perhaps reducing immigration rates by half, perhaps by more.

But a sustainable immigration policy would slow immigration without scapegoating immigrants. Blaming immigrants is not only mean-spirited but spurious. Indeed, in environmental terms, all northwesterners should be more like recent immigrants; immigrants do less harm to the Northwest environment than do native-born residents or domestic migrants. In general, first-generation immigrants do not live in big houses, drive sport utility vehicles, or engage in recreational shopping. It is not until the second generation that immigrants' consumption rates typically reach those of the general population.[113]

Again, the issue is immigration, not immigrants.

TAKING CARE OF
OUR OWN

WHAT WILL THE PACIFIC NORTHWEST be like in 2020—some two decades after Charlie Langdon testified at Representative Cook's welfare hearings, Paige Latin spoke with yet another group of teenagers, and Chuck Carpenter introduced House Bill 3070? How many of the teenagers Paige spoke to will have teenage children of their own? Will llamas still graze near the Sisters of Saint Mary's land, or will it have become another subdivision full of two-legged transplants from other, even more crowded places?

By 2020, will the region's population grow by 41 percent, as official projections forecast, rising to 21 million and squeezing more additional people into the bioregion than now live in Washington? Will communities continue to be destabilized by unrelenting mobility—a mobility encouraged by taxpayer subsidies? Will wages for the North American poor continue to be pushed downward—and will the global poor be left to languish—because of high-paced international immigration into North America? Will half of the American women who need them still lack access to public family-planning services? Will the curse of sexual abuse still descend each year on a tenth of young people? Will northwesterners continue to tolerate a status quo in which wealth of unprecedented magnitude accrues to the fortunate while every seventh child lives below the lowest poverty line in the Western world?[114]

An oddsmaker from another planet might answer these questions, "Yes, probably. The Northwest will likely go the way of many other places. Distrustful of its public institutions and unable to rouse itself before it is overwhelmed by physical, social, and environmental decay, the Northwest will be trapped by its own misconceptions."

But northwesterners, through their actions, may instead answer the questions with a resounding "No!" Capitalizing on hopeful signs already appearing—declining birthrates, slowing mobility, gradually diminishing immigration—they may create a different future. They may expose the roots of population growth like so many weeds in a field and then reap an unexpectedly full harvest: stronger communities, more secure childhoods, more productive and peaceful citizens, safer streets, less pressure on the environment, and—in the end—an uncrowded home place. They may show the world that when you take good care of people, population growth takes care of itself.

Charlie Langdon, Paige Latin, Chuck Carpenter, and thousands of others are already hard at work in that field. The question is, Who will join them?

NOTES

The Pacific Northwest includes British Columbia, Washington, Oregon, and Idaho in their entirety. It includes Del Norte, Humboldt, Mendocino, Siskiyou, Sonoma, and Trinity Counties in California and Deer Lodge, Flathead, Granite, Lake, Lincoln, Mineral, Missoula, Powell, Ravalli, Sanders, and Silver Bow Counties in Montana. It also includes the Alaskan boroughs of Haines, Juneau, Ketchikan Gateway, Sitka, and Yakutat and the Alaskan census areas of Prince of Wales–Outer Ketchikan, Skagway-Hoonah-Angoon, Valdez-Cordova, and Wrangell-Petersburg.

Most of the population data cited in this book were drawn from several large spreadsheets developed at Northwest Environment Watch (NEW) between 1993 and 1997. These spreadsheets—which detail population trends, birth and death rates, domestic migration rates, immigration rates, and birthrates among different age goups—were assembled from a large number of sources, most of them originating from either the national census programs of the United States and Canada or the national and state programs for collecting vital statistics. Some extrapolation was needed to complete the spreadsheets, particularly for early years.

To contact the people mentioned in this book:

- Advancing Solutions to Adolescent Pregnancy
  172 20th Avenue
  Seattle, WA 98122
  Tel. (206) 323-1107

- Prostitution Alternatives Counseling and Education
  P. O. Box 73537
  1014 Robson Street
  Vancouver, B.C. V6E 1A7
  Tel. (604) 872-7651

- Representative Chuck Carpenter
  H-493 State Capitol
  Salem, OR 97310
  Tel. (503) 986-1407

1. Mike A. Males, *Scapegoat Generation: America's War on Adolescents* (Monroe, Maine.: Common Courage Press, 1996); Kristin Luker, *Dubious Conceptions: The Politics of Teenage Pregnancy* (Cambridge, Mass.: Harvard Univ. Press, 1996).

2. Social science findings summarized in Luker, op. cit. note 1.

3. Share of teen mothers who are poor from Alan Guttmacher Institute (AGI), *Sex and America's Teenagers* (New York and Washington, D.C.: 1994).

4. Poverty as root problem from Males, op. cit. note 1; Luker, op. cit. note 1.

5. Growth due to teen births from sources cited in note 23.

6. Total fertility rates from B.C. Ministry of Finance and Corporate Relations, *British Columbia Population Forecast Update* (Victoria: 1996); Washington Office of Financial Management (WOFM), *1995 Population Trends for Washington State* (Olympia: 1995); Center for Health Statistics, *Oregon Vital Statistics Annual Report 1994* (Salem: Ore. Dept. of Human Services, 1996); and Center for Vital Statistics and Health Policy, Idaho Dept. of Health and Welfare, Boise, private communications, June 1997.

7. Poverty-fertility link from, among others, Males, op. cit. note 1; Luker, op. cit. note 1; and Amara Bachu, *Fertility of American Women: June 1992* (Washington, D.C.: U.S. Bureau of the Census, 1993).

8. Luker, op. cit. note 1.

9. Share of fertility caused by poverty estimated, among others, from Mike A. Males, School of Social Ecology, Univ. of Calif., Irvine, data analysis for NEW, May 1997; from Bachu, op. cit. note 7; and from comparisons of Northwest fertility rates with fertility rates in low-poverty industrial countries, reported in Lee Rainwater and Timothy M. Smeeding, "Doing Poorly: The Real Income of American Children in a Comparative Perspective," *Luxembourg Income Study Working Paper No. 127* (Syracuse, N.Y.: Syracuse Univ., 1995), and Population Reference Bureau (PRB), *1995* and *1996 World Population Data Sheet* (Washington, D.C.: 1995, 1996). Ratio of childbearing by class estimated from Bachu, op. cit. note 7; and T. J. Mathews and Stephanie J. Ventura, "Birth and Fertility Rates by Educational Attainment: United States 1994," National Center for Health Statistics, Hyattsville, Md., April 24, 1997.

10. Federal funding cuts from James McIntire et al., "Policy Choices for Working Families in Washington," Fiscal Policy Center, Univ. of Wash., Seattle, March 1997. Income losses from U.S. welfare cuts from Urban Institute analysis, cited in Peter Edelman, "The Worst Thing Bill Clinton Has Done," *Atlantic Monthly*, March 1997. Washington welfare grants and "standard of need" from Children's Budget Coalition, "1997–1999 Biennial Budget Request," Seattle, Jan. 1997.

11. State-by-state benefits from Annie E. Casey Foundation, *Kids Count Data Book 1996* (Baltimore, Md.: 1996). Poverty line compared with other nations from John L. Palmer et al., eds., *The Vulnerable* (Washington, D.C.: Urban Institute Press, 1988). B.C. benefits from Karen Johnston, Communications Dept., B.C. Ministry of Human Resources, Victoria, private communications, May 1997. European benefits from Rainwater and Smeeding, op. cit. note 9.

12. Northwest growth rate from sources cited in note 13; North American growth rate and global growth rate from PRB, *1995* and *1996 World Population Data Sheet* (Washington, D.C.: 1995, 1996). Rankings among states from Edwin R. Byerly and Kevin Deardorff, *National and State Population Estimates: 1990–1994* (Washington, D.C.: U.S. Bureau of the Census, 1995). B.C. ranking from sources in note 13.

13. Northwest states population over time (and Figure 1) from the following sources produced by U.S. Bureau of the Census in Washington, D.C.: *Current Population Reports*, Series P-25, Nos. 139, 304, 460, 957, 1106, and 1127 (various years); *Current Population Reports*, Series P-26, Nos. 85-CA-C, 85-MT-C, 85-AK-C, and 88-A; *Population of Counties by Decennial Census: 1900 to 1990* (1994); Population Estimates Branch, "July 1, 1990 to July 1, 1994 Population Estimates for Counties," 1995; and recent Web data (http://www.census.gov/). B.C. population from data provided to NEW by B.C. Statistics, Victoria, drawn from Statistics Canada, Canadian Socio-Economic Information Management System (CANSIM) Time Series Data Base.

14. Distribution of population from sources in note 13.

15. Figure 2 from sources in note 13 and from B.C. Ministry of Finance, op. cit. note 6; WOFM, op. cit. note 6; Paul R. Campbell, *Population Projections for States, by Age, Race, and Sex: 1993 to*

2020 (Washington, D.C.: U.S. Bureau of the Census, 1994); B.C. Ministry of Health and Ministry Responsible for Seniors, *The Nineteen-Eighties: A Statistical Resource for a Decade of Vital Events in British Columbia* (Victoria: 1994); Center for Health Statistics, *Oregon Vital Statistics Annual Report,* Vol. I and II (Salem: Ore. Dept. of Human Services, various years); Glenda Larson, analyst, Center for Vital Statistics and Health Policy, Idaho Dept. of Health and Welfare, Boise, unpublished data, Oct. 10, 1995.

16. Current generation as 2,000th assumes modern humans began about 40,000 years ago and that each generation spans 20 years. World population trends from, among others, Marion Carter, demographer, PRB, Washington, D.C., private communication, Dec. 4, 1995.

17. Human protoplasm from Edward O. Wilson, "Is Humanity Suicidal?" *New York Times Magazine,* May 30, 1993. Terrestrial plant matter from Peter M. Vitousek et al., "Human Appropriation of the Products of Photosynthesis," *Bioscience,* June 1986. Water use from Sandra L. Postel et al., "Human Appropriation of Renewable Fresh Water," *Science,* Feb. 9, 1996.

18. Forests from Sandra Postel and John C. Ryan, "Reforming Forestry," in Lester R. Brown et al., *State of the World 1991* (New York: Norton, 1991). Grasslands from Till Darnhofer, deputy director, Desertification Control Program Activity Center, United Nations Environment Programme, Nairobi, Kenya, private communication, May 23, 1991. Extinction rate from John C. Ryan, *Life Support: Conserving Biological Diversity* (Washington, D.C.: Worldwatch Institute, 1992). Chemicals in our bodies from Theo Colburn et al., *Our Stolen Future* (New York: Penguin, 1996).

19. John C. Ryan and Alan Thein Durning, *Stuff: The Secret Lives of Everyday Things* (Seattle: NEW, 1997).

20. Seattle land area from Puget Sound Water Quality Authority, *State of the Sound: 1992 Report* (Olympia: 1992); Montana, Idaho, and Oregon land area from U.S. Dept. of Agriculture, Natural Resource Conservation Service (NRCS), published and unpublished data from the National Resources Inventories of 1992, 1987, and 1982 provided to NEW by each state's NRCS office. Driving from Alan Thein Durning, "Vehicles Outnumber Drivers in Pacific Northwest," *NEW Indicator,* Jan. 1995.

21. Consumption of energy and emissions of carbon dioxide from NEW database as reported in John C. Ryan, "Greenhouse Gas Emissions on the Rise in the Northwest," *NEW Indicator,* Aug. 1995. Solid waste from Wash. Dept. of Ecology, "Solid Waste in Washington State: Fourth Annual Status Report," Olympia, Feb. 1996; B.C. Ministry of Environment, Lands, and Parks, Municipal Waste Reduction Branch, "B.C. 1994 Municipal Solid Waste Reduction Data Summary Report," Victoria, Aug. 1995; and Ore. Dept. of Environmental Quality, "1994 Oregon Material Recovery Survey," Portland, 1995. Water consumption from, among others, B.C. Round Table on the Economy and the Environment, *State of Sustainability* (Victoria: Crown Publications, 1994).

22. Carlyn E. Orians and Marina Skumanich, "The Population-Environment Connection: What Does It Mean for Environmental Policy?" Battelle Seattle Research Center, Dec. 1995.

23. In Figure 3, "unplanned" refers to births resulting from pregnancies unintended at the time of conception. "Births" are births in excess of deaths. Deaths were subtracted proportionately from planned and unplanned births. An alternate calculation, which subtracted all deaths from planned births, revealed that unplanned births equal 70 percent of natural increase. Migration figures represent net migration. "Domestic migration" was calculated as total migration minus immigration. Immigration data based on people born citizens of a foreign country, not on direct immigration to Northwest during specified period. Components of growth and Figure 3 from sources in note 13 and the following: additional data on total natural increase from Center for Health Statistics, *Washington State Vital Statistics 1994 & 1995* (Olympia: Wash. Dept. of Health, 1996), and Center for Vital Statistics and Health Policy, *Idaho Vital Statistics* (Boise: Idaho Dept. of Health and Welfare, various years). Teen births from National Center for Health Statistics, *Vital Statistics of the United States:* Vol. 1, *Natality* (Hyattsville, Md.: various years); Wash. Dept. of Health, *Pregnancy & Induced Abortion Statistics 1995* (Olympia: 1996); unpublished data from Pat Starzyk, Center for Health Statistics, Wash. Dept. of Health, Olympia, Oct. 10, 1995; and Division of Vital Statistics, *Selected Vital Statistics and Health Status Indicators, Annual Report* (Victoria: B.C. Ministry of Health and Ministry Responsible for Seniors, various years). Shares of

unplanned births, by age, from Institute of Medicine, *Best Intentions: Unintended Pregnancy and the Well-Being of Children and Families* (Washington, D.C.: National Academy Press, 1995). Immigration from U.S. Bureau of the Census, *Census of Population, Vol. I, Characteristics of the Population,* parts for Washington, Oregon, Idaho (Washington, D.C.: U.S. Government Printing Office, various years); Gary Alampi, ed., *Gale State Rankings Reporter* (Detroit: Gale Research Inc., 1994); Kristin A. Hansen (Population Division, U.S. Bureau of the Census), "Profile of the Foreign-Born Population in 1995: What the CPS Nativity Data Tell Us," paper presented at Population Association of America annual meeting, New Orleans, La., May 9, 1996; Statistics Canada, *1981 Census of Canada, Place of Birth, Citizenship, Period of Immigration* (Ottawa: Minister of Supply and Services Canada, 1984); and Statistics Canada, *1991 Census of Canada, Immigration and Citizenship* (Ottawa: Minister of Industry, Science, and Technology, 1992).

24. Share of unplanned pregnancies from Institute of Medicine, op. cit. note 23, and Laurie Cawthon, "First Steps Database: Family Planning," Wash. Dept. of Health, Olympia, Sept. 1995.

25. "Teen mothers" are mothers aged fifteen to nineteen; "school-age mothers" are mothers aged fifteen to seventeen. Teen births and rates from sources in note 23.

26. M. Males and K. S. Chew, "Adult Involvement in School-Age Fertility," paper presented to Population Association of America annual meeting, San Francisco, April 8, 1995, cited in Males, op. cit. note 1.

27. Income trends from Robert H. Frank and Philip J. Cook, *The Winner-Take-All Society* (New York: Free Press, 1995). Median earnings of high school graduates and dropouts from Casey Foundation, op. cit. note 11.

28. Income trends from Edward N. Wolff, *Top-Heavy: A Study of the Increasing Inequality of Wealth in America* (New York: 20th-Century Fund Press, 1995); and Daniel H. Weinberg, *A Brief Look at Postwar U.S. Income Inequality* (Washington, D.C.: U.S. Bureau of the Census, 1996). U.S. income equality compared with other countries from Rainwater and Smeeding, op. cit. note 9.

29. Canadian middle class defined as people in households earning between 75 and 150 percent of median income, from Michael

Wolfson, "Trends in Economic Inequality in Canada, or 'Stasis Amid Change' Revisited," presentation to CIAR/Health Canada Conference, Toronto, Oct. 30, 1995, cited in B.C. Ministry of Health and Ministry Responsible for Seniors, *A Report on the Health of British Columbians: Provincial Health Officer's Annual Report 1995* (Victoria: 1996).

30. Violence rates from Howard N. Snyder and Melissa Sickmund, *Juvenile Offenders and Victims: A National Report* (Washington, D.C.: Office of Juvenile Justice and Delinquency Prevention, U.S. Dept. of Justice, 1995), and Howard N. Snyder et al., *Juvenile Offenders and Victims: 1996 Update on Violence* (Washington, D.C.: Office of Juvenile Justice and Delinquency Prevention, U.S. Dept. of Justice, 1996). Child abuse from Andrea J. Sedlak and Diane D. Broadhurst, "Executive Summary of the Third National Incidence Study of Child Abuse and Neglect," National Center on Child Abuse and Neglect, U.S. Dept. of Health and Human Services, Washington, D.C., Sept. 1996. Drug abuse from Carnegie Council on Adolescent Development, *Great Transitions: Preparing Adolescents for a New Century* (New York: Carnegie Corporation, 1995).

31. Child poverty rates for Northwest states, based on children aged five to seventeen living in a parent's household in 1993, from U.S. Bureau of the Census, Small Area Income and Poverty Estimates Program, posted on Web (http://www.census.gov/). B.C. child poverty rate, for 1995, from Statistics Canada, *Low-Income Persons, 1980 to 1995* (Ottawa: 1996), converted to the American standard based on data in Rainwater and Smeeding, op. cit. note 9. European child poverty rates from Rainwater and Smeeding, op. cit. note 9.

32. Share of poor who are children from Luker, op. cit. note 1. Chronic poverty from Cassandra Burrell, "Study: 48% in Chronic Poverty Are Children," *Seattle Times,* Aug. 19, 1996. International comparisons from Rainwater and Smeeding, op. cit. note 9. Seniors lifted out of poverty from William P. O'Hare, "A New Look at Poverty in America," *Population Bulletin* (PRB, Washington, D.C.), Sept. 1996.

33. Mosler quoted in Males, op. cit. note 1.

34. Myth of work as cure for poverty and earnings of welfare recipients from O'Hare, op. cit. note 32. Northwest poor children

in families with working parents from Casey Foundation, op. cit. note 11. Nonworking welfare recipients as parents from McIntire et al., op. cit. note 10.

35. Disabilities from Edelman, op. cit. note 10. Duration of poverty and reasons for falling into poverty from Palmer et al., op. cit. note 11.

36. Males, op. cit. note 1.

37. Males, op. cit. note 1; Luker, op. cit. note 1.

38. Males, op. cit. note 1.

39. Arline Geronimus et al., "Does Young Maternal Age Adversely Affect Child Development? Evidence from Cousin Comparisons in the U.S.," *Population and Development Review*, Sept. 1994.

40. Birthrates and poverty rates from Seattle–King County Dept. of Public Health, *Lost Youth: Teen Pregnancy and Birth in King County* (Seattle: 1994). Abortion rates from Luker, op. cit. note 1, and AGI, op. cit. note 3.

41. Teen births, a five-year average for 1991–95, from Center for Health Statistics, *Washington State Pregnancy and Induced Abortion Statistics 1995* and *Washington State Pregnancy and Induced Abortion Statistics 1991–94* (Olympia: Wash. Dept. of Health, 1996). Child poverty from U.S. Bureau of the Census, op. cit. note 31.

42. Teen births, a five-year average for 1991–95, from Center for Health Statistics, *Oregon Vital Statistics Annual Report 1991, 1992, 1993, 1994,* and *1995* (Salem: Ore. Dept. of Health, various years). Child poverty from U.S. Bureau of the Census, op. cit. note 31.

43. Teen births, a five-year average for 1991–95, from Julie McDonald, medical consultant, Vital Statistics Agency, B.C. Ministry of Health and Ministry Responsible for Seniors, Victoria, private communications, May 1997. Poverty rate from Ministry of Health, op. cit. note 29.

44. NEW compiled data on teen births and child poverty for all American counties in the Pacific Northwest. The data included five-year average teen birthrates for 1991–95 from Center for Health Statistics, op. cit. note 41; Center for Health Statistics, op. cit. note 42; Center for Vital Statistics and Health Policy, *Annual Summary of Vital Statistics* (Boise: Idaho Dept. of Health and Welfare, various years); Children Now, *California County Data Book 1995* (Los Angeles: 1995); Family-Planning Section, *Trends in*

Montana Teen Pregnancies and Their Outcomes: 1981–1995 (Helena: Mont. Dept. of Public Health and Human Services, 1997); and Institute of Social and Economic Research, *Kids Count Alaska Data Book 1996* (Anchorage: Univ. of Alaska, 1996). They also included poverty rates from U.S. Bureau of the Census, op. cit. note 31.

Researcher Mike A. Males of the School of Social Ecology, University of California, Irvine, calculated the correlation between poverty and teen births. The correlation was statistically highly significant (0.43), and for the 15 most populous counties, it was nearly one to one (0.91). NEW also compiled five-year average teen birthrates for 1991–95 for each of 20 B.C. health districts (from McDonald, op. cit. note 43) and compared them with a composite poverty indicator created by the B.C. Ministry of Health (Ministry of Health, op. cit. note 29). B.C. does not track poverty rates at the health district level but constructs a poverty indicator from three closely related measures: the percentage of the population receiving public income assistance, the unemployment rate, and the share of people aged fifteen to twenty-four who have less than a ninth-grade education. The Ministry ranked the health districts from best to worst on each of these measures, then summed the three ranks for each district. Thus, a district that ranked first on each of the three measures would have an overall poverty indicator score of three. Analyzing these data, Males found another strong correlation (0.87) with birthrates. A data supplement to this book is available from NEW and at NEW's Web site; it contains teen birth and child poverty rates for each county or health district.

45. Bachu, op. cit. note 7.
46. Mathews and Ventura, op. cit. note 9.
47. Births by age from Mike A. Males, School of Social Ecology, Univ. of Calif., Irvine, private communication, May 19, 1997.
48. Casey Foundation, op. cit. note 11.
49. Never-wed teens with support awards from Rebecca A. Maynard, ed., *Kids Having Kids* (New York: Robin Hood Foundation, 1997). Payment amounts from O'Hare, op. cit. note 32. Washington child support due from Rachel Zimmerman, "Watch for License Law on Child Support," *Seattle Post-Intelligencer,* Jan. 22, 1997.
50. California study cited in Males, op. cit. note 1.

51. Palmer et al., op. cit. note 11; Males, op. cit. note 1.

52. Palmer et al., op. cit. note 11; Males, op. cit. note 1.

53. Because prison data are not kept by county, NEW calculated prison population to include Alaska and Montana but not California (which alone has 143,000 people behind bars) from Bureau of Justice Statistics, *Correctional Populations in the United States 1985* (Washington, D.C.: U.S. Dept. of Justice, 1986); Mark Carnopis, public information officer, Idaho Dept. of Corrections, Boise, private communication, March 28, 1997; Perrin Damon, communications manager, and Karla Younessi, communications intern, Ore. Dept. of Corrections, Salem, private communication, April 14, 1997; Wash. Dept. of Corrections Web page (http://www.wa.gov/doc/); and Kent Nugen, project manager, Stafford Creek Correctional Center, Wash. Dept. of Corrections, private communication, April 1, 1997.

54. Expansion projects and plans from sources in note 53.

55. State education spending from Wash. Office of Financial Management, unpublished data, Olympia, June 1997.

56. Jonathan Kozol, *Amazing Grace* (New York: HarperPerennial, 1996).

57. Share of female abuse victims from Michele D. Wilson and Alain Joffe, "Adolescent Medicine," *Journal of the American Medical Association,* June 7, 1995.

58. Past sexual abuse among prostitutes, as stated by Paige Latin, from Badgely Commission, *Sexual Offenses against Children and Youth* (Montreal: Queen's Printer, 1985), and Sue Currie, *Assessing the Violence against Street-Involved Women in the Downtown Eastside/Strathcona Community* (Vancouver: B.C. Ministry of Women's Equality et al., 1995).

59. Sedlak and Broadhurst, op. cit. note 30.

60. Washington Alliance Concerned with School-Age Parents (WACSAP, now Advancing Solutions to Adolescent Pregnancy), "Breaking the Cycle: A Handbook for Educators Working with Sexually Abused Teen Mothers," Seattle, undated; Debra Boyer et al., *Victimization and Other Risk Factors for Child Maltreatment among School-Age Parents* (Seattle: WACSAP, 1992).

61. Authority-figure rape from survey conducted by *Los Angeles Times,* cited in Males, op. cit. note 1, and from Sedlak and Broadhurst, op. cit. note 30.

62. Ages of rape victims from study conducted by National Victim Center, cited in Males, op. cit. note 1. American and Canadian rape rates from U.N. Economic Commission for Europe, cited in Robert Evans, "Rape, Murder More Prevalent in U.S.," *Seattle Post-Intelligencer,* Dec. 13, 1995.

63. Growth in abuse reports from the Kids Count state data book program of the Annie E. Casey Foundation of Baltimore, Md.; Children First for Oregon, *County Data for Community Action: 1996 Status of Oregon's Children* (Portland: 1996); Children Now, op. cit. note 44; Idaho Kids Count, *1996 Profiles of Child Well-Being* (Boise: Mountain States Group, 1996); Institute of Social and Economic Research, op. cit. note 44; Montana Kids Count, *1996 Data Book* (Helena: Montana Coalition's Healthy Mothers, Healthy Babies, 1996); and Wash. Kids Count, *State of Washington's Children 1996* (Seattle: Human Services Policy Center, Univ. of Wash., 1996). Growth in abuse reports and share of reports investigated from Sedlak and Broadhurst, op. cit. note 30.

64. Share of school-age mothers abused from Boyer et al., op. cit. note 60. Share of teen girls abused from Wilson and Joffe, op. cit. note 57, and from survey conducted by *Los Angeles Times,* cited in Males, op. cit. note 1.

65. Boyer et al., op. cit. note 60.

66. Boyer et al., op. cit. note 60.

67. Boyer et al., op. cit. note 60.

68. Share of abused school-age moms with multiple births from Boyer et al., op. cit. note 60. Share of teen births that are repeat births from Luker, op. cit. note 1. Reproduction seen as cure from WACSAP, op. cit. note 60, and Males, op. cit. note 1.

69. Males, op. cit. note 1.

70. Chances of abuse and abduction from Sedlak and Broadhurst, op. cit. note 30, and David Finkelhor et al., *Missing, Abducted, Runaway, and Throwaway Children in America* (Washington, D.C.: U.S. Dept. of Justice, 1990). State of denial from Richard N. Brandon et al., "Developing a Communications Strategy for Protecting Children," Human Services Policy Center, Univ. of Wash., Seattle, Feb. 1996.

71. Unwanted and mistimed pregnancies from Institute of Medicine, op. cit. note 23, and Cawthon, op. cit. note 24.

72. Unintended births by characteristics of mother from Institute of Medicine, op. cit. note 23; explanation from Luker, op. cit. note 1.

73. Unintended birth trends from Institute of Medicine, op. cit. note 23, and Cawthon, op. cit. note 24. International comparisons from Elise F. Jones et al., "Unintended Pregnancy, Contraceptive Practice, and Family Planning Services in Developed Countries," *Family Planning Perspectives,* March/April 1988.

74. Stephen Matthews et al., "The Effects of Economic Conditions and Access to Reproductive Health Services on State Abortion Rates and Birthrates," *Family Planning Perspectives,* March/April 1997. Women in counties without abortion providers from S. Henshaw and J. VanVort, "Abortion Services in the United States, 1991 and 1992," *Family Planning Perspectives,* May/June 1994.

75. Institute of Medicine, op. cit. note 23. Washington unintended pregnancies avoided from Community and Family Health, *Benefit: Cost Analysis of Family Planning in Washington State* (Olympia: Wash. Dept. of Health, 1994).

76. Success of publicly funded family planning from Luker, op. cit. note 1. Public support for family planning from poll conducted by Lake Research for Planned Parenthood Federation of America, Washington, D.C., April 1996.

77. Federal funding cuts from AGI, op. cit. note 3. Federal spending per capita is for Idaho, Oregon, and Washington; state-by-state spending from Terry Sollom et al., "Public Funding for Contraceptive, Sterilization, and Abortion Services, 1994," *Family Planning Perspectives,* July/Aug. 1996.

78. Washington service shortfall from Community and Family Health, op. cit. note 75. Companies active in contraceptive research from Deborah L. Shelton, "The Revolution ... that Never Happened," *American Medical News,* April 15, 1996.

79. Lauran Neergaard, "Birth Control for 'Morning After' OK'd," *Seattle Post-Intelligencer,* Feb. 25, 1997.

80. Cost-effectiveness from James Trussel et al., "The Economic Value of Contraception: A Comparison of 15 Methods," *American Journal of Public Health,* April 1995. Washington contraceptive coverage from Wash. Office of Insurance Commissioner, "Data Call Summary: Women's Health Issues," Seattle, 1996. National data from AGI, *Uneven & Unequal: Insurance Coverage and Reproduc-*

tive Health Services (New York and Washington, D.C.: 1993).

81. Impact on population growth of reducing unintended births modeled by NEW based on Institute of Medicine, op. cit. note 23, and on data from sources cited in note 23.

82. Northwesterners' places of birth from U.S. Bureau of the Census Web data (http:\\www.census.gov\) and Statistics Canada, *1991 Census of Canada, Immigration and Citizenship* (Ottawa: Minister of Industry, Science and Technology, 1992). Reasons for moving from Larry Long, *Migration and Residential Mobility in the United States* (New York: Russell Sage Foundation, 1988); Don McRae, "Economic Impacts of Population Change: Part One" (prepared for the B.C. Round Table on the Environment and the Economy), Statistics Branch, Ministry of Finance and Corporate Relations, Victoria, Nov. 1992; and from Gundars Rudzitis et al., "Public Views on Public Lands," Dept. of Geography, Univ. of Idaho, Moscow, Nov. 16, 1995.

83. Domestic migration's share of growth from sources in note 23. Income of migrants from Long, op. cit. note 82.

84. High North American mobility from Patricia Gober, *Americans on the Move* (Washington, D.C.: PRB, 1993). U.S. moving rate from Kristin A. Hansen, *Geographic Mobility: March 1993 to March 1994* (Washington, D.C.: U.S. Bureau of the Census, 1995). Counties' changeover from Michael Irwin et al., "How to Build Strong Home Towns," *American Demographics,* Feb. 1997.

85. Social impacts of mobility from Gober, op. cit. note 84, except income inequality from William Frey, "The New White Flight," *American Demographics*, April 1994.

86. Hansen, op. cit. note 84. Jean Dumas and Alain Bélanger, *Report on the Demographic Situation in Canada 1995* (Ottawa: Statistics Canada, 1996).

87. Dumas and Bélanger, op. cit. note 86.

88. Irwin et al., op. cit. note 84.

89. Legal protections from McRae, op. cit. note 82, and ECO Northwest, *Evaluation of No-Growth and Slow-Growth Policies for the Portland Region*, prepared for Metro, Eugene, June 1994.

90. Background on growth boundary from Mary Kyle McCurdy, 1000 Friends of Oregon, Portland, private communication, April 15, 1997.

91. Mary Webber, Metro, Portland, private communication, April 15,
     1997.
92. Eben V. Fodor, "The Real Costs of Growth in Oregon," Energy
     and Environmental Planning Associates, Eugene, July 1996.
93. Metro, "Urban Reserves: Frequently Asked Questions," Web site
     (http://www.multnomah.lib.or.us/metro/growth/).
94. SIP from Ore. Economic Development Commission, *An Analy-
     sis of the Impacts of Industrial Investment Property Tax Incentives in
     Oregon* (Salem: 1996). Washington tax breaks from Hal Spencer,
     "Manufacturers Get Tax Break," *Seattle Times,* March 30, 1996.
95. Skilled-labor shortage from Howard Wineberg, "Oregon's Mi-
     gration Patterns: A Note on the Recent Mix of In-migrants
     and Out-migrants," *Northwest Journal of Business and Economics,*
     1996. Job growth from Fred Klatz, Ore. Employment Dept.,
     Salem, private communication, May 23, 1997. Population
     increase from Ore. Economic Development Commission, op. cit.
     note 94.
96. ECO Northwest, op. cit. note 89. The effects of raising devel-
     opment fees are unknown because it is unclear whether higher
     fees would reduce new housing supply enough to raise housing
     prices across the board (which would be detrimental to current
     residents, especially the poor), mostly dissuade migrants from
     coming, or mostly suppress land prices.
97. Long, op. cit. note 82.
98. Long, op. cit. note 82. Noneconomic reasons for moving from
     Thomas M. Power, *Lost Landscapes and Failed Economies: The Search
     for a Value of Place* (Washington, D.C.: Island Press, 1996), and John
     Young, chairman and chief executive officer, Hewlett-Packard,
     presentation at Greater Seattle Chamber of Commerce, Lead-
     ership Conference, Coeur d'Alene, Idaho, Oct. 18–19, 1993.
99. Pacific Northwest economic performance from Thomas M.
     Power, "Economic Well-Being and Environmental Protection
     in the Pacific Northwest," *Illahee: Journal for the Northwest En-
     vironment,* fall/winter 1995.
100. Some international immigrants move directly from a foreign
     nation to the Northwest; others land elsewhere in the United
     States or Canada first and later relocate. Approximately 8 per-
     cent of foreign-born residents of B.C. are American, some from

Northwest states; likewise, some immigrants to the Northwest states come from B.C. The figures used in this book have not been adjusted to reflect these within-Northwest flows of international migrants. Immigrants in Northwest from sources in note 23.

101. North American share of all international immigrants from Philip Martin and Jonas Widgren, *International Migration: A Global Challenge* (Washington, D.C.: PRB, 1996).

102. James P. Smith and Barry Edmonston, eds., *The New Americans* (Washington, D.C.: National Academy Press, 1997).

103. George J. Borjas, "The New Economics of Immigration," *Atlantic Monthly,* Nov. 1996.

104. B.C. as destination for newcomers from Citizenship and Immigration Canada, *Annual Report to Parliament: Immigration Plan 1994* (Ottawa: 1994). Foreign-born percentage from Statistics Canada, op. cit. note 82.

105. Share of U.S. Northwest population that is foreign born from U.S. Bureau of the Census, *U.S. Census of Population:* editions of *1950, 1960, 1970, 1980,* Vol. 1, *Characteristics of the Population,* parts for Washington, Oregon, and Idaho (Washington, D.C.: U.S. Government Printing Office, 1952, 1963, 1973, 1983), and Alampi, op. cit. note 23. Geographic distribution of U.S. immigrants from President's Council on Sustainable Development, *Population and Consumption Task Force Report* (Washington, D.C.: 1996.)

106. William H. Frey, "Immigrant and Native Migrant Magnets," *American Demographics,* Nov. 1996.

107. Washington from William Frey, "The New White Flight," *American Demographics,* April 1994; Oregon from Wineberg, op. cit. note 95.

108. Dumas and Bélanger, op. cit. note 86; Citizenship and Immigration Canada, op. cit. note 104; Martin and Widgren, op. cit. note 101.

109. Rosemary Jenks, "Immigration Reform Moves through Congress," *Immigration Review* (Center for Immigration Studies, Washington, D.C.), winter 1996.

110. David North, *Soothing the Establishment: The Impact of Foreign-Born Scientists and Engineers on America* (Lanham, Md.: Univ. Press of America, 1995). Foreign medical students from Steven

Findlay, "AMA Group: Trim Foreign Med Students," *USA To-day*, Feb. 26, 1997.

111. Canadian industries from Don DeVoretz, Simon Fraser Univ., Vancouver, B.C., cited in Douglas Todd, "The Case for Controlling Immigration," *Globe and Mail*, Feb. 1, 1997. Effects on high school dropouts from Smith and Edmonston, op. cit. note 102.

112. Geographic distribution of illegal immigrants from President's Council, op. cit. note 105.

113. Consumption patterns among immigrants from Orians and Skumanich, op. cit. note 22.

114. Projected population from Campbell, op. cit. note 15, and Ministry of Finance, op. cit. note 6. Family-planning services from President's Council, op. cit. note 105. Sexual abuse rate from Wilson and Joffe, op. cit. note 57. Child poverty rate from sources cited in note 44.

Alan Thein Durning is founder and executive director of Northwest Environment Watch and author of books including *This Place on Earth, The Car and the City,* and *How Much Is Enough?* Formerly a senior researcher at Worldwatch Institute, he lectures widely but lives in the city where he grew up.

Christopher D. Crowther is a research intern at Northwest Environment Watch and will soon be pursuing graduate studies in demography at the University of California, Berkeley. He has contributed research to other NEW publications, including *The Car and the City,* and he worked as a VISTA volunteer for an adult literacy nonprofit organization. Chris is a confessed interstate migrant.

Northwest Environment Watch is an independent, not-for-profit research center based in Seattle. Its mission: to foster a sustainable economy and way of life throughout the Pacific Northwest—from southern Alaska to northern California and from the Pacific Ocean to the crest of the Rockies.